Straight

(A novel in the Irish-Māori tradition)

By

Michael O'Leary

Earl of Seacliff Art Workshop
Paekakariki 2015

978-1-86942-159-5

PROLOGUE

Paul Calvert woke about an hour out of Auckland on a train journey back from dreamland. Tired, slightly nauseous. Will this travel never cease? He thought, because he didn't want it to. Will this railway soon finish? He wished it wouldn't! It was early in the morning as the train passes through station after station. Knowing it isn't long before arrival, melancholy floods him, brought on by a mixture of memory, the landscape and the motion of the train: together these create a kind of perfection like lovemaking which he knows must end.

Papakura Station, newly painted and dripping with dew, is a peaceful welcome to the Auckland boundary. Calvert had a warning that Papakura was up ahead twenty miles or so before when he had passed through a cutting and the earth was red with a topping of bright green grass against a dark blue sombre sky. He thought 'papa kura: soon we'll be in Papakura'. Papakura Station stands still as his train moves slowly out and he catches sight of a suburban train filling with early morning commuters on the far platform which will follow his train into Auckland in ten minutes or so. These are things that will happen but Calvert is dreaming...*in dreamland, te wahi moemoeä, horrific transvestite fear over the strait, I am my mother dying...I fly in an ever-encircling stranglehold moving towards the ceiling...looking down I can see myself...tobacco-picking job doesn't begin...I leave for the darkness of self-absorption...an overnight stay lasts two weeks and a girl with a name like Rhodesia talks me down...*passing Middlemore Hospital Calvert is now almost awake as the train moves lazily towards Mangere.

The dining car normally closes north of Papakura but he manages to persuade the people in it to give me a cup of coffee. This is his first trip to Auckland from dreamland for some time. Hoping he has left dreamland for good this time, Calvert is unsure what he will do from now on. There will be no one to meet him at the station. He has been away so long that all his northern friends have either dispersed or forgotten him, and his family who are in Auckland don't know him since he went into the exile of te wahi moemoeä.

"He kura kanga e hokia, he kura tangata e kore e hokia," As his carriage passes over the points near Westfield which take the train onto the Waterfront-Orakei Deviation, Rangi's last words to him ring in his ears, each word punctuated by the boom-cha-boom, boom-cha-boom of the train. Only now as he enters excitedly the outskirts of his childhood haunts does he begin to understand the explanation of her ancestral proverb. Fighting off illusions and tiredness he attempts to reach a fuller comprehension of what she'd meant by saying, 'You can return to a treasured place, but not to a treasured person', From the train window he catches a glimpse of ghetto-like Glen Innes, spread out like a ragged carpet, spread out like an inaccurate map of his past. Paul Calvert knows he is almost home - not the home of people, but the home of places and ghosts and memories...*in the dream I was sitting on a sofa in the house of an old friend with the improbable name of Shamus O'Shamus...we had met up in dreamland after not seeing each other for some time...she walked in on our literary language, it was Rangi, my never-to-be-wife, kahore täku hoa wahine...our eyes met without fear and our hearts wanted to run away with each other...things are never simple in dreamland and she left me desolate ...still she haunts all my* dreams and I love her like the moment I met her...*when the darkness descends she is there telling me how you can never return to a treasured person* ...Paul Calvert notices the carriage has gone dark. It is eerie when another train going the other way blows its whistle and rushes by inside the double-track tunnel, sounding like a resurrected dinosaur hearing itself roar for the first time in two million years.

The train emerges from the tunnel out into Meadowbank and Calvert feels torn from every side by emotion. Memory-images of the past are before him as though they are here, palpable! The train goes faster but for him it has stopped! It moves but doesn't move! Up to the right he can see the church which was part of his old school. Two horses run down the hill as the train frightens them and he is a nine year old boy looking down through the bushes which surround his school. Calvert can see the early morning train from Wellington that he is now on rumbling along the tracks and two of the horses that belong to the rich kids at his school are running down the hill, they must be scared. The time-train passes under the Orakei overbridge as it moves through Orakei Station, and he can see the mysterious gin factory to the left - he could never believe that that's what it was when he was young because he thought all things like that came from overseas.

Well this train moves...*in dreamland trains move...if they move at all it is through the efforts of our labour...before Rangi arrived, before the cold set in...before the fire of ice burned my heart to a frozen cinder...in this land I helped to keep the trains going...going through tunnels and climbing steep gradients...when no trains came we would dig and lift and heave ho!...hey-up!, hey-up!, hey-up!...another sleeper lies in a ballast bed...replace that rail up at 339 was the order of the day...and how can a man work wearing two coats, eh Flook!!!...pipi and paua sizzling on a shovel...*but these dreams detract from immediate emotions for here he is on a train going through his home and all he can do is dream.

Orakei, Calvert struggles to understand the meaning of the word, but the train is moving again for him. He can see the old sewer pipe he and other kids used to walk across to Parnell and back. Parnell Baths, Judges Bay pass without comment and the train becomes entwined in the mesh of rails that is the Auckland rail yards, slowing to a crawl as an early goods train heads out of the yards, southbound, two engines pulling fifty or so wagons...*my brother has just laughed himself to sleep in the bed next to me... we stay up till late talking and laughing..."Don't shoot, I've got six wives and a children" and we both roar our heads off...mum calls out "Shut-up you two, go to sleep!"...now he is asleep and mum and mad and the two girls asleep in the next room, and gran asleep in the front room...not me, I lie awake in the dark, I don't like to sleep because you don't know anything...but as I lie in the dark I can hear the steady rumble and drone of a goods train going through the night...through Orakei Station...I don't care where it goes but that sound haunts and terrifies me...if it wasn't for that sound I wouldn't know I was alone...I want mum to come in and put her arms around me and say it's all right...she used to but now I'm too big...*

CHAPTER 1

The train jerks to a halt at Platform 4 of Auckland Station. Calvert is quite awake now but prefers to watch the people pour out of the carriages rather than make any definite movement himself. Big greetings and meetings, hongi and handshakes are being exchanged, kisses and hugs. Bleary-eyed, up-all-night travellers meet their friends and loved-ones - this is what a railway station should be like, Calvert thinks to himself. So many more Māori and Polynesian faces here than in dreamland, to the south. A little girl wanders past the carriage window and for the time he thinks "a little Rangi Brown!" - this simple sentence recurs almost daily after he's been in Auckland for some time. So, he might see a small Māori girl anytime and he will think "a little Rangi Brown" and will be both upset and reassured.

Finally, everyone has left the train and the workers are rushing through each carriage retrieving hired pillows and emptying rubbish containers. Calvert tells them he is vacating the carriage, gathers his meagre belongings, steps down from the train, and heads for the cafeteria to get a kai and settle his thoughts about what to do now he has arrived.

After a somewhat frugal breakfast of soup and toast and a cup of coffee, Paul Calvert gets on a bus that will take him to town. Auckland Railway Station is a metaphorical gauge for Auckland City as a place, that is, it stops short of the mark. So, as the station stands aloof and beautiful, fronted by large Phoenix palms lending it an air of exotic colonialism, this station doesn't quite go to the centre of the city. And the city itself doesn't quite have a heart, a focal point where people can say they are in the heart of the city. Queen Street is more like a man-made Grand Canyon than a valley where people settle for shelter and protection...*on a Friday night after school Paul Calvert would gather the kids together and get the bus to town...they would all go to the movies and then meet mum about 7pm outside her work...she had a cleaning job because their dad was in prison down south...we would all have tea and then mum and the kids would go home...I would stay in town to meet school friends outside 246 or just look around the record shops and music shops...a couple of years later I bought an electric guitar which was really neat but I had to take it back when dad got sick because mum needed the money..."Hot town Summer in the City" was blaring on the radio and I used to pretend I was a bohemian (long before I learned the meaning of the word) grooving around the 'Village' in New York, and there I was walking up Queen Street on a Friday night before all the big buildings went up, but it seemed so much bigger then and "times were very hard when I was young"...*as the bus moved off from the Station Calvert realised that it was not a trolley-bus as it would have been before he left for te wahi moemoeā. This puzzled him and made him sad, but he soon enjoyed the sharp precision and smooth modernity of the Mercedes as it swung into Queen St. from Customs St., without the age-old fear of the trolley poles flying off the overhead wires. Queen St. looked much the same, if anything the addition of several larger buildings made it appear sparser and smaller than it did in the old days.

Getting off the bus at Vulcan Lane, which had been paved over and turned into something of a mall or at least a walkway, since the dream-time, Calvert went into one of the pubs in the Lane, ordered a drink and sat down..."*hōmai te inu-ahi!*" *cried Golliwog as he snatched a bottle of whiskey from my hand in one of the city of dreams...I gave him a wry "Kia ora," as he swallowed a quarter of the bottle in one gulp..."Wha, wha, what are you doin' here, e hoa" Golliwog said to me..."Ha, ha, how did you get to dreams" he asked...when I told him I had flown there he believed me and burst out laughing..."Si, si, so did I" he said, handing me back my whiskey...*that was in dreams but here he was sitting opposite Paul Calvert in a pub in Vulcan Lane, in Auckland in reality.

"Tena koe! Kei te pēhea koe, e hoa?"

It was Golliwog sitting sober and sane opposite Calvert reading a newspaper.

"Kei te pai," Paul answered, and they sat talking quietly. Calvert had never seen him in te wahi moemoeā except when he was really out of it. It was good to see him now, especially since Calvert was feeling lonely and a bit subdued, a stranger in a familiar land.

However, several drinks and several pubs later Golly, as Calvert had always called his friend, had fixed him up with a job and a place to stay for a few days. Paul could work with him, he said, laying kerbstones and doing a bit of drainage work, and he went away to ring his boss to confirm that Calvert would start tomorrow. Calvert became a bit anxious when he heard Golly, whose real name was Hone, arguing and shouting over the phone. He was afraid that not only had he not got him a job, but had caused himself to get the sack. But Hone returned smiling.

"You gotta job, start Monday"...*in dreamland one day Golly had gone to get paua off the rocks - dream rocks - near where we lived...he returned with a sack of paua but seemed somewhat perturbed..."I was nearly killed" he said, "nearly fell a hundred feet to the rocks"..."I'll get you a whiskey, haere ki te moe"...after a couple of hours sleep his kaha returned and he spent the rest of the evening making paua fritters...*"Hey Hone, do you remember the time you went on that paua hunt?" Paul said rather drunkenly.

"No" Hone replied, "let's go!"

Paul Calvert wakes but doesn't know where he is. It is almost light, there is someone moving about in the room and he knows it isn't him. He can't move! He can't do anything except feel pain. What a hangover! "Oooh Aaah!" he groans.

"Teach you to get so haurangi, eh!" said the voice from the person who was doing the moving around. It is Golly's sister, Hine, it must be her room he's in. He realises he is lying on the floor next to her bed, no wonder he was so cold.

"Boy, you fellas was drunk last night. You kept trying to get into bed with me, and I kept throwing you out, it was funny, eh!"

"I must have been drunk," Paul said, "to want to sleep with you." She threw a hairbrush at him and walked out.

"You can get into my bed now," she called from the kitchen. "You want a cup of tea, you haurangi rat"...*I slipped off to dreamland and there was Rangi...I used to tease her: "Poor Rangi, she's a porangi"...she'd get angry and I'd say "Brown,* funny name for a Mäori"...she'd throw something at me then laugh..."Here's your tea. I got to go

to work now," said Hine. "See you later, good to see you, eh."

She gave him a kiss on the forehead.

"Good to see you too," Calvert called after her. Then he could feel the bruises from falling on the floor after being kicked out of bed. He grimaced and fell asleep in Hine's bed...*in dreamland we walk down the main street of the stone city...your young daughter is up on my shoulders..."Look Mum look!" she cries, at anything that moves...her fingers fold over my eyes like night flowers covering my view of already dark dreaming skies..."Hey! I can t see!" I cry out and she laughs and takes her fingers away...looking down the old main street...looking northward I can see the hill which dominates the cityscape...it is said that the rise of the hill is the puku of a Mäori chief lying on his back...the day is cold and calm and there is mist on the hill...tomorrow it will probably snow...the colours in the sky are stark and austere...in dreams you are beautiful and dreamland mirrors your beauty...we are a family yet not a family and being apart sometimes crushes me...we are going to the grand old hotel for lunch where the man plays piano in the corner...across the table, good food, good wine...your little girl talks on to herself while we talk...*"Wake up! wh, wh, wake up!" yells Golly in my ear.

"Come on, man, let's go downtown, here's a coffee. You seen Tania and her daughter lately by the way?"

Paul mumbles no and drinks the coffee, feeling physically and emotionally drained. Hone and Paul walk from his place in Ponsonby to the bus stop. Calvert is still a bit out of it, slightly confused. Ponsonby looks as though it's changed since he has been dreaming and it is now several years since he's lived there, although, as usual, things seemed only like yesterday.

Places around Ponsonby looked familiar, yet a lot newer, as though there had been an earthquake or a war and the people had wanted to completely restore the suburb the way they remembered. Only in doing so the whole character of the place had changed. As they walked past the recently painted houses and shops which now stocked patê, salami and brie, Calvert had a kind of a reactive twinge, a repulsion that one gets when one knows something has changed irrevocably.

"Bit different now, eh" says Hone as they stood waiting for the bus. When the big yellow banana bus arrives Calvert is again reminded that the trolley buses are gone from Auckland streets. Ponsonby Road just doesn't seem the same without the overhead wires which used to dominate the skyscape. His instinct is to immediately retreat to the never-changing beauty of dreamland, he finds his mind is slip-sliding into the mire of melancholy memory but he fights it.

"Mind over memory" Calvert says to himself. Unfortunately, he says this just as he is boarding the bus. The driver looks at him in a suspicious tone and he has to recover quickly and say,

"Two to the city," handing him the money...*they hand him the money and he gives them a week's supply of smack...it will probably only last the night and they will survive another week by stealing and ripping each other off...if you look closely you can see the handle of the revolver the dealer carries in a shoulder* holster...now that he has hit everyone up he leaves this run-down, rodent-infested house in a no-exit Ponsonby cul-de-sac...as the dealer drives off in his Jaguar it doesn't take much to think that in ten years when I return from dreamland he will own a similar house, fully restored and be a respectable restaurateur, while most of the junkies in Hippie Hotel will be dead or in the bin or jail..."Ten years have passed, ten years with the length of ten Indian summers!" Calvert thinks aloud. Hone interjects with a witty, smiling

"Inflation has even hit poetry, I see!" and they both laugh. As the bus turns into K. Road Calvert gets a kind of thrill, like seeing an old friend.

Karangahape Road, the deformed relative of Auckland's main street, Queen Street, which is middle-class and well-dressed. K Road, as it is known, would more aptly be called Queen Street because it harbours most of the seedier side of Auckland. This is where the trans-sisters, pimps and prostitutes ply their wares. K Road where all the bordellos and massage parlours entice the suspecting gentlemen off the streets to taste the delights of people who have expensive tastes.

It is also a lively area by day, the main shopping area for the multicultural inner city dwellers. As the bus turned left into Queen Street, Hone, who had been prattling on incessantly up till now, suddenly went quiet.

"Anything wrong?" Paul asked him.

"Maybe, Professor!" It was strange hearing Hone call him by his old nickname he hadn't heard for years; it made him think how long they'd known each other.

"I just saw a couple of cops talking to my brother, Skids!"

"Boy! Is Skids old enough to be in trouble with the law?" Paul mused. Golly grinned at him, and then went serious.

"They are probably just giving him a talk about sniffin' in public or something. Anyway, nothin' we can do. If we get off they'll be gone one way or another. You know, that young Skids, he's a bit of a hero around town. We all laugh at home, eh, because he's got the mana to be at the top because the streetkids think that his name Skids is short for streetkids. We all tease him if we're at home for a kai on the weekend or something. Mum hits him over the ear and says 'You gotta do the dishes Skids, mana or no mana.' And my young sister says he only got called that because he kept skidding over when he was still about eight, when everyone else could walk properly and everyone laughs"...*Shamus O'Shamus and I had stalked the streets all night...earlier we were out of it and smoking on the last bus to Ponsonby...the big Māori lady driving the bus turned around and said in a gruff voice, 'Hey you put that thing out! Or I'll put you out!'...we sat somewhat subdued, slightly paranoid until the trolley bus went around a sharp corner and the poles went flying off the wires...this was too much for Shamus and he burst out laughing uncontrollably...I soon followed and we both were hysterical by the time the driver got back from fixing the poles...she threw us off the bus, the zoo bus, the last bus to Ponsonby, and we walked, stalked the streets ending up at Mothers, a cafe run by a burly transvestite...O'Shamus ordered a doughnut and a coffee and Raylene made a joke about the jam in the middle...*"We're here," said Golly. They got off the bus and walked to the downtown Queen Elizabeth Square.

"I'll just go an' ring Auckland Central Pig-sty to see if they picked up Skids." While Calvert waited for Hone he just looked around the square. All the new buildings were so tall compared with those in dreamland. The old Dilworth Building, while over-towered by the new neighbours was strangely enhanced by them all. He looked up at the Central Post Office and then remembered the toy shop that used to be across the road...*mum, can I have that articulated truck for Christmas, can I, please...You'll have to ask Santa that dear, she answered...I said yes but I couldn't understand why mum winked at the man behind the counter...we went outside where the tramlines were being ripped up...I liked the trams, the way they used to clink along the middle of the road...mum, why are those men taking the trams away...I don't know, dear, come on let's go...I didn't say any more about the trams because mum looked just as sad and puzzled about them as I was...I went back to wondering whether Santa would give me the white truck*..."Remember the old fleapit!" said Hone.

"What," Paul said, realising that Golly was back.

"The old Oxford theatre that was here before that Downtown thing."

"Yes, I do," he said, "but I only went once. How's Skids?"

"They never got him, just a warning, the pig gave me a lecture on being his older brother and all that and said I should do something before he gets into real trouble. I told him I got enough worries and besides I said Skids is the one who bosses me around these days. The cop said fuck off and hung up. Where you wanna go now, eh!"

It was nearly lunchtime so Calvert suggested they go and meet Hine. They walked around the corner into Customs Street then up to Fort Street where she worked in a lunch bar. Walking past the Star building Calvert could see before him the towering Roller Mills Company...*in dreamland there is a brewery which is built on a steep hill...it is old and looks quite Dickensian...it is an intriguing area when you walk in dreams and smell the hops...this dream-city has many strange distinctive smells which dominate certain areas like sacred ancient territorial rites and sites...sometimes things become white and cold, other times black and cold*..."Youse boys are up early" calls Hine as she sees them. The threesome made their way up Emily Place towards a small coffee shop at the elbow of the road. As they walked past the Japanese Bath House Golly called out "Arse Oh!" and they all laughed.

"I didn't know you could speak Japanese, brother," said Hine.

"Yeah!" said Golly, "I learned it on TV". They were still laughing when they entered the coffee house...*in dreamland, if I remember rightly...you had to go downstairs to the coffee club...you could meet anyone there...Beaconsfield often dropped in for a dram...anyone could belong to the coffee club...'percolated egalitarian' we used to call it...I remember going down there to tell you I love you...but it wasn't me, it was artificial, bad-timing...you turned away and I was weakened and whakamā...'Can I have a milk-shake, mummy' said your little girl...'Christ! she's beautiful, black and strong!' Iggy Pop mirrored on the radio*..."Well, I must be going back to work," said Hine. "You can sleep in my bed tonight long as you behave!"

"Let's have a drink!" said Golly as he and Paul eventually left the elbow room. They walked down Shortland Street and came to Vulcan Lane from the back way where they went into a bar and ordered a couple of large beers and sat down.

They sat drinking for a while, talking, smoking, looking and listening. At length the bar began to fill, all sorts of people pouring in after their various daily battles...*I tried to think of my father and his daily battles...I never knew my father and the man I called my father was actually my stepfather...my mother conceived me in Germany, where she had gone after the war to be a nurse...while assisting in the rehabilitation of the country she also helped in the rehabilitation of my father...at the age of seventeen I found out my step-father wasn't my father...I always felt, since I can remember, a darkness, a guilt-edge to my life, an inherited demon, as though the sins of my father were visited upon me...I remain in the dark...*"It's getting dark out there," said Golly.

"What's that!" Paul Calvert said, confused.

"Night outside!"

"Oh yeah," he said. By now the pub was almost full. People were in groups of four or five or more talking about this and that and everything.

"Won't your boss be annoyed that you didn't go in today, Hone?"

"No, he knows you're here. He'll understand. He'll be pleased I've got a man like you to start work on Monday!" Then, suddenly, Hone's mood went angry.

"My father was in the Māori Battalion in the desert war," said Golly. "He used to tell me that despite the whole terrible time of the war, the years of fighting and deprivation, the dead comrades, the worst thing he ever experienced, far worse than anything fucking Rommel dished up, occurred on the ship on the way back, eh. When the troop ship called into South Africa on the way back from war the Pākehā soldiers all went on shore leave. But, the Māori Battalion was not allowed on the fucking shore 'cos of the colour of their skin. He hated the Pākehā more than the Germans"...*I've got a photo of my father...it is all I know of him...he is wearing a uniform which looks very nice. It is a black uniform and has a silver leaf on one lapel. This is my real father...I found this photograph when I found my mother dead one morning...*"Another drink Paul," said Golly.

As Hone left for the bar, Calvert noticed a familiar face. He wasn't sure at first, it had been at least ten years, but as he watched further he realised it could be no other.

"Tony Blunt! You bastard!" Calvert called in a loud voice. Blunt, somewhat taken aback and obviously embarrassed, looked sheepishly around.

"Calvert! Paul Calvert!" he cried out, losing all formality when he saw who it was. "How the hell are you?"

Blunt excused himself from a group of rather stunned young lawyers with whom he had been conversing, and made his way over to their table. Hone had returned and the three of them sat, introduced Blunt and then started into a conversation...*our conversation ended unsatisfactorily...I had asked my step-father whether the photo I found on my mother's body was my real father...in the end, because of his evasion and hurt I could only assume that it was...he kept saying over and over how his brother Roy, my uncle (presumed) had been shot down by the Germans, how his own life had been destroyed by the war...I said I understood this but I still had to know who this man was who wore two lightning stripes on one lapel...*"I was defending a member of one of your old gang the other day" Blunt was saying to Golly.

"Calvert, old boy," said Blunt switching his keen intelligent eye to Calvert, "Have you still got that wacky idea that your father was a Nazi? Remember how we all used to have you on about that at university?"

Paul Calvert could see Golly's eyes goggle, this was a part of his friend's life of which he knew nothing. A few hours and many drinks later Golly and Calvert left the pub because it was after closing time and the Manager was raving on about the cops closing him down if we didn't leave etc, etc. They Jingled through their pockets as they sauntered up Queen Street hoping to find enough for a couple of hamburgers and a taxi back to Ponsonby.

Despite the amount they'd had to drink they were both still quite sober. Hone turned to Calvert as they passed 246.

"What did that Blunt mean when he said your old man was a Nazi?"

"It's a bit difficult to explain. My father, the one that you knew, wasn't my real father. He was the father of the rest of the kids",...*but when they got married mum had just got back from Germany and she was already pregnant with me...mum got off the train with me inside her...he was there at the station...'I said I'd wait for you darling' said my presumed father...'Oh Rich, how am I going to tell you. I thought about it all the way back on the boat from England, and last night on the train from Wellington - I'm pregnant'*...In the taxi Golly was still asking Paul about his father and mother. He was intrigued and as incredulous as Calvert himself was. Calvert told him most of what he knew was conjecture. When they walked in his front door he said, "Weird, man!"

Hine was already asleep when Paul got into bed beside her. He was as quiet as he could be and she just murmured a night noise without waking. He had slept with her many times before but never any more than just sleep in the same bed. She was like a sister to him. Although thoughts of love-making flashed through his mind as he felt her warm body next to him there was never any question that they were any more than like brother and sister. Hine turned towards Paul and he fell asleep in her arms...*te wahi moemoeä...the place of dreams where Rangi was with me...she was real and I didn't know - I was in my mind and thought she was too...yet there was Rangi beside me, wanting me and I was afraid...intimacy was too much, direct expression of love was beyond my dreams...I made excuses and gave reasons against the reality of life...to Rangi and to myself I was untrue...now I am alone at night when once she was with me...when I'm with a new lover I want her to be Rangi and love is destroyed...I know the price of everything and the value of nothing without being a cynic...in dreamland I found reality, now I am lost in reality my dreams crush my heart...'As soon as I saw her I knew she would hurt you', said my friend George...te wahi moemoeä, the place of dreams...te wahi kuku, to pö te pö te pö nui...*"Are you awake?" Paul heard Hine softly say. She was crying quietly. It must have been the middle of the night, and the mixture of darkness and drunkenness and Hine's tears and his own darkness conspired to make him realise he didn't know where he was.

Hine held Paul close not saying anything, just crying softly. They made love gently and after Hine had gone to sleep he lay awake for a while. He could hear a truck grinding up nearby College Hill and the first light was beginning to show on the wall. He closed his eyes and saw Rangi's face. It was a skull, and Paul Calvert fell into an uneasy sleep.

"Wake up! Wake up!" Hone was shaking him excitedly. "It's that Blunt fella on the phone, he says he's gotta talk to you in a hurry."

As Calvert got out of bed he noticed Hine give him a curious look and turn away. Tony Blunt's educated voice came crystalline over the phone.

"Morning Calvert, sorry to get you out of bed at the ungodly hour of midday, but I've been doing a bit of detective work and I think I've stumbled onto something rather amusing, if not to say interesting, concerning your heritage. I don't want to talk over the phone. Can we meet in Albert Park, say, in an hour?"

Calvert mumbled something which must have approximated 'yes' because he said "Oh! Jolly good, I'll see you by the band rotunda"...*by the band rotunda we used to go...she was a little bird and I was Mr. Tree...she would sit in my branches and tell me of her marvellous travels and I would be a place of rest for her...'Oh! Mr. Tree,' she would begin 'if you could only fly'...we were both artists and people would not believe what we told them...I would walk her to her bus and she would be off to the surreal suburb and I would go back on the trolley-bus to Ponsonby and continue the painting of her I was doing from a photograph...other people would look say 'I can't see a bird or a tree'...*"Where are you going, come back to bed!" Paul heard Hine order him. He tried to explain about meeting Blunt but she turned away.

"Go away! You all the same."

"I'll be back in a couple of hours", but she was crying and angry.

"Don't bother. If you not here when I need you then I don't want you. Get another bed tonight."

Out on the street Calvert walked in an obsessive fit of rage and incomprehension. "Blunt better have something good!" he hissed to himself. His thoughts of Hine were less rational, swaying from 'that bitch' to 'what a bastard I am to leave.' He crossed the lights at Three Lamps almost without looking to see if anything was coming, and had stomped half way down College Hill before he even thought of catching a bus. He might as well continue walking he thought, as he didn't know the time-table and it was a Saturday. As he reached the top of the rise of Victoria Street West he could just make out the time on the University clock tower which rose above the trees of Albert Park like the peak of an ivory mountain out of the clouds. It was five to one so Calvert ran down the hill, crossed Queen Street and into Victoria Street East in what seemed like one gigantic stride, then into the quaintness and tranquillity of the Park itself.

"Ho there, Calvert" called Tony as Calvert headed towards the bandstand.

"This had better be good Blunt," he said. He was more angry at Hine than him and after he'd caught his breath and calmed down Blunt and Calvert settled into the familiarity of a close, long-lasting friendship. For although they hadn't seen each other for many moons and their lives had gone in completely different directions, they had known each other and supported each other through a time in both their lives which was crucial to their individual intellectual and emotional development. In short, they had known each other better than brothers.

Tony pulled out a curious-looking, slightly yellowing volume from his bag. He handed it to Calvert, saying "Page 31 will probably interest you." The title of this puzzling book was *The Journal of Esoteric and Antiquated Linguistics*, Berlin 1938, English Language edition. Paul Calvert turned to page 31, and what he saw just about stopped the flow of blood through his heart. He couldn't speak, move, do anything but stare at the half-page photograph...*in dreamland there was a film made of a man eating a woman's face, which was on the back of her head...'I'll photograph it now', said John the Photographer...I was the man and Rangi was the woman and I was trying to impress her...I wanted her to be my love and as I ate her polystyrene face off the back of her beautiful black hair I was sure it wouldn't be long before I'd be making love to her...this was in dreams and we were playful and new and free with each other...it was before the storm clouds gathered sending us for shelter in different directions...*"Well, what do you think of that eh, Calvert?" Blunt asked.

"It certainly explains a few things," Paul said, "but it raises a thousand more questions than it answers. I'm completely stumped Tony!"

The photograph Blunt had shown him was of three men in their mid-twenties. They were all intelligent and successful-looking, and all were studying linguistics and. were in Berlin for a conference. One was Roy Calvert, Paul's uncle, who was giving a paper on the work he was doing at Cambridge. Another was his presumptive father, Richard Calvert, who was apparently studying ancient Gaelic scripts at Trinity College, Dublin, something which he had kept from his family during all those years of Paul's growing up with him. But the third man was the one who knocked him, for it was the same man in SS uniform as Paul had seen in the photograph he had found on his mother's dead body.

It was his actual father. His name was Helmut von Klagen and, according to the article, he was studying ancient Nordic scripts at Munchen University, with a view to discovering origins of Aryan superiority in the legends of the past. At this point Tony Blunt, sensing his friend's inability to comprehend this knowledge, said

"Let's go downtown and find a bar. I've got a few embellishments to add to this little story."

As they walked out of Albert Park Calvert caught sight of a late model black Mercedes Benz coming very slowly down Bowen Avenue. It passed them at the Victoria Street intersection, then it seemed to speed up and was out of sight before he could mention it to Blunt.

"Come on, old man, Mercedes are two a penny in Auckland these days. Even the buses are Mercedes, you're letting this thing get the better of you already. Next thing you'll be saying you've been conscripted to invade the Sudetenland!" Blunt said in his affectionate, sarcastic style of speaking...*after school we used to have running battles with the kids from the State school...*"Catholics, Catholics ring the bell. Protestants, Protestants go to hell!!!!" *our leaders, who were always the girls, would yell out...monkey apples and bits of dirt would be flying through the Orakei air...twenty or thirty kids in a running battle, flailing school bags, rulers* for swords...mayhem in the suburbs, once a site of wars...wars of colonisation...tribal wars of revenge and conquest...Ngäti Whätua land, Crown land...State housing side by side with the country's richest real estate...clay fights down by the footy club...challenge and defend...got ya, you're dead!...bang, bang, bang..."Another brandy Calvert," said Blunt. "Thanks!" his friend replied. Blunt came back with a couple of large drams.

"Now to continue", Blunt said, after a quick swig. "This presumed father of yours seems to be a bit of a wag. While studying at Trinity he was actually using his position to procure arms from Germany for none other than the illustrious I.R.A. He would make those excursions to the Fatherland under the protection of his esteemed brother's academic reputation, himself being no mean scholar it must be noted. And this von Klagen chap whom you claim was your father, was his contact. Extraordinary don't you think?"...moemoeä, the elephants' graveyard, Hine nui te pö sits in waiting...I met, or someone met a priest who told him, 'te wahi o te tonga' that's the place where the bad spirits of the European war go'...the 'death's head' people live out their hell in the

minds of the living...you must be strong if one enters your heart for they want you to be like them in a dream reality...they are the evil of old and want you to despair...move, and never rest, ngä mökai, for they will call you and you will be alone..."Excuse me, Tony I must make a phone call."

"That you Hone?" Paul said.

"What you want, man, you really got my sis mad. She's been porangi all day. What did you do, fuck you?"

"Tell her I want to talk to her." He heard Hone shout something.

"She don't wanna talk to you".

"Tell her if she doesn't come to the fucking phone I'm coming around".

"What you want creep, eh!" Calvert heard Hine's accusing voice coming through the bit of moulded plastic.

"I want to see you," he said, all his anger and resistance had left. He felt threatened and naked in his spirit, he simply wanted to see her. "I'll meet you in the bar at the back, the quiet one, eh?"

"You better have a good story" she said, but now she spoke without bitterness and hung up gently.

Tony had got them another cognac each and was sitting twirling his glass in his fingers holding it up to the light, watching its amber colour change shades.

"Curious how I came across this really, Calvert. I first saw that photograph five or six years ago when I was on that post-graduate scholarship to Cambridge. You may remember, I did my doctorate on the linguistics of legal language. I just happened to be flicking idly through old journals one afternoon and I came across that photograph of your father and your uncle. Of course I never connected that von Klagen chap with what you used to tell us about your father being a Nazi. I thought that was just a razz. Then the other night in the hotel when you showed me that picture that your mother had left I was a bit taken aback, but I wanted to be sure. So, I kept quiet and when I got home I looked up the journal which I planned to give you anyway. The rest, as they say, is history."

"How did you know Golly's phone number?" Calvert asked Blunt.

"Oh! Don't you remember scrawling it on the back of a newspaper the other night. Really old man!"

"Well, what do I do now?" Paul Calvert addressed the question half to Blunt and half to myself...*'I don't know,' said mum. 'Aw mum, you must know if you've got Mäori blood in your side of the family'...'Yeah mum!' said my little sister...'Well I think we've got a bit. You know Gran escaped from the Tarawera eruption when the pink and white terraces got buried'...'Dad always says you're a Maori, mum!'...'Dad says, you're like the Maoris, you don't know whether you're laughing or crying'...'What does dad mean by that, mum?'...'That little Maori boy Taffy - Sammy's brother - died last week, mum! I really wanted to go to his funeral up in the Mäori houses up at Boot Hill...'Will Taffy be in heaven with our sister, mum'...mum said yes dear and turned away and made a funny noise like laughing or crying...*"Well, we know your physical father survived the war, you're the living proof of that. I wonder if von Klagen stood trial for war crimes? Of course, just being in the SS meant he was deemed a criminal against humanity. Anyway, Paul, on Monday I'll go to the university History department and check up a few things. O Lord, I'd better go, my wife and I are off to see the opera tonight. My life won't be worth living if I'm late."

"Thanks very much for turning my whole life upside down!" Paul said. "Seriously, I don't know what to do now."

"Just let it ride till I find out a few things on Monday, and give me a call on Monday evening. No, better still here's our address, come around for dinner on Monday evening."

After Blunt left Calvert sat staring into his empty glass for a few minutes, then he got up and walked down Queen Street to where he said he'd meet Hine...*te wahi moemoeä ...in the dark dream place I was jealous...I rumbled through the town like a tank...I pounded every shop window with my fist until one gave way and shattered like crystal in the night...I screamed out her name in a drunken fog...she went home and I went into the pub...I drank like a fish and swam home...I woke up beside her in the middle of the night...I asked my beautiful flaxen-haired dream lover what had happened...she told me and we laughed and then made love...*"So there you are."

"How are you, Hine?" Paul asked.

"Pretty hoha" she replied. But she kissed him.

"Let's go and have a kai after we've had a drink and I'll tell you what's come up," he said, still unsure of her mood.

"Ai," she said. She seemed exhausted and exasperated at once. Then she said, "Hömai te inu-ahi."

Paul smiled as he walked to the bar. This was the kind of private joke that develops between people who have known each other or of each other for many years. It was their name for whiskey and was one of the jokes that Golly and he had worked out using slight shifts in their two languages. Now these had become part of Hine's vocabulary too and it bound them together...*'Kia Ora begorrah to the Mäori Irishman O'Calvert'...'Arahonui, e hoa big balls!' thus Golly and I greeted each other as we prepared for a day of loading railway wagons...all day the trucks came in with goodsfor the rail and I would direct them where to go, which wagon, then back to my book...Golly and I would go over to the bus terminal for lunch, then to the pub, the early opener where we used to go years before after being turned down yet again for sea-gulling...Calvert O'Calvert the Irish Catholic with the Protestant name; his father he was orange and his mother she was green...haere ki te mahi before it's time to go home...*"And now I find out my father was running guns for the I.R.A." Calvert muttered to himself.

"I beg your pardon sir?" the barman said.

"I said two double whiskies, one straight and one with ginger ale and ice, didn't you bear me?"

Hine and Paul walked quietly across Queen Elizabeth Square. They were going to eat at the cafe in the old Ferry Buildings, walking slowly, holding hands and not saying anything. As they stood waiting for the 'Cross Now' at the Quay Street lights Hine was singing a little tune to herself; the sky was just beginning to darken to a deep blue in the east, a few seagulls flew overhead looking like blithe spirits against the evening. Just as they were about to step out off the footpath a late last-minute car came roaring along past the big red gates of Queen's Wharf. Calvert thought it was just someone trying to beat the red light, but just before it got alongside them it slowed to a virtual crawl and someone in the back seat pointed something at them. Paul's first thought was a gun! He pushed Hine to one side and then fell to the ground rolling over as he did so.

"He's got a gun, run!" Paul screamed to Hine. After what seemed an age he realised that he was still alive and that their 'assassins' had disappeared in the twilight, but he had recognised the car was a black Mercedes like the one earlier in the day.

"What was that about, you bloody porangi," Hine screamed at him.

"I'm sorry!" he said. "It must have been a camera not a gun."

"Fuck, man! You crazy - a gun! - a camera! What is this?" She started crying and when he touched her she pushed at him violently.

"I can explain, it's all connected with that stuff this morning, I think. I don't even know myself what's going on. I thought they were trying to kill us - me, at least - and I pushed you away so you wouldn't get shot. Oh Christ, Hine! Listen, I don't even know what's happening, who they are or anything. Stop crying will you please and I'll tell you what I know - I'm upset too"...*Tania was dead too, when she was young...she told me the story as we left her sister's place in Eden Terrace and walked across the footbridge that leads to Mt Eden Station...she said she was thirteen and she lived in dreamland and was in a car accident...the doctor said she was dead but she was just at the valley of the dead, standing on the big rocks overlooking her ancestral Ngä Puhi people...some old kuia stayed at the gate to give the karanga to those who wanted to enter after they died ...they saw Tania walking towards them but instead of giving her the call one of them said 'Go back daughter, you are not ready, haere atu'...then she woke up and people who thought she was dead told her and she said yes, 'but I was told to return'...then the early afternoon train came and I loved her more than ever...I said to her it was a good thing we didn't sleep together the other night when we had been out of it...but I didn't believe it and neither did she and the train became a relentless metaphor of movement and regret...*Hine and Paul stood there under the remorseless, unseen gaze of the Māori Chief statue. 'If only he would speak and tell us what to do', Paul Calvert thought.

"If his balls were really frozen like I read about in a poem, he wouldn't be so smug," Calvert said after a long silence.

"God, you Pākehā - can't you say or do anything sensible?" said Hine with a faint smile. "Come on," she took him by the arm and they crossed Quay Street. As they entered the cafe, which felt so warm and inviting after our tête-à-tête with the Mercedes, Paul Calvert suddenly felt shattered.

"Hine, I don't know what's going on!"

"You sit down Paul, I'll get us a coffee. You wanna order a kai now?"

"No! Leave it till after I've told you what Tony said, I couldn't eat now anyway!"

Hine sat listening to his story, which was half explanation to her and half working it out in his own head. She sat silently, no expression on her face to give Paul an indication of how she felt. At once he felt drawn to her as though they'd been lovers for years, and very distant from her as though she was a new kind of life-form and he didn't know how to react to it or how it would react. At length he concluded his tale of two fathers, or what he knew of it, and Hine got up without saying a word, went to the counter and ordered two coffees and came back and sat drinking in silence. After what seemed an age, but was only five minutes or so, Hine stood up as if to leave. Paul was almost ready for a big scene, but she just said softly,

"Come on Paul, drink your coffee, I'll shout you a dinner on the Kestrel." He was so relieved, and he suddenly felt both happy and hungry.

"Hurry up," she called to him from the cafe door, "it's leaving in five minutes!"

They walked quickly past the closed bookstall to the ticket office...*I remember going with dad in our Morris van down to get the vehicular ferry to Birkenhead...'There's always such a big queue these days, it'll be a godsend once the bridge is finished'... I sat on the bonnet as we approached Northcote Point and I looked up at the half-finished panacea for Auckland's projected development and I thought there was something amiss ...the North Shore always appeared rather unnatural to me...no railway lines and all that bush and dirt roads...the vehicular ferry looked like a flattened-out submarine and I would pretend it was a U-boat like in the war comics...'Can we go and see our cousins with the big verandah and all the toys, dad please?' 'Not today' my presumed father answered, a hurt in his tone that I never understood till much later...*"What a lovely night," said Hine as they stood on the top outside deck of the Kestrel, the only remaining 'real' ferry left in Auckland.

As the boat rounded the end of the wharf and headed out across the harbour towards Devonport they could see a few ships anchored in the stream waiting to go into port to unload. It was almost full moon and moonbeams danced and shimmered on the sparkling waters. The stars and the lights of the receding city gave a kind of coloured spotlight effect. Hine held his hand and they embraced and were contented with each other and the night.

Descending the staircase to the on-board café, Hine said "Boy, I'm so hungry I could eat a horse!"

"I don' t think they're quite sophisticated enough for your tastes here, could have something to do with there not being enough room below," he teased her. She hit him over the ear and said,

"What do you want for a kai, imbecile?" They ordered and then sat down...*in the snow-covered lunar-like landscape of central dreamland we sat down among the ruins of dreaming ghosts of gold-diggers...our dark coats contrasted with the white blanket of snow that surrounded us and enhanced my feeling of melancholy and inspiration...under normal circumstances I should have felt wretched...my blond-haired young lover, the one I had dreamed of as I put my fist through a drunken cold night window, was with me...'I don' t think we should be lovers any more' Miranda said softly, turning her head to the dreamlike sunset as we sat together, yet apart, on stone upon stone rubble of a past era, an hotel of Winter's dream...as soon as I asked why I realised it was no good asking...the sky turned turquoise from blue over the white, white landscape and Miranda's words had made me feel alone and overwhelmed...I didn't understand and I knew that this coming night would be our last...it was magic, dream-like far away long ago and yet the world was so beautiful although I could no longer touch it...*"Well, what we gonna do?" asked Hine. "I don't wanna get in just another bloody fucked up relationship," she said. "I like being with you Paul, eh, and I would like to be with you some more but I'm bloody hoha with going from one to the other, you know."

"Yes, I know how you feel, Hine, I'm sick of this bloody modern love we're all caught up in. It's easy and it's fun for a while but you know something's missing! I've got to find a place to stay in the next couple of days, so when I start the job on Monday I'll be able to feel a bit on an even keel."

Hine leaned over and put her hand on his wrist. "Come and sleep with me tonight, e Paul, please, then we can work it out from there, Kei te anake au." He could feel her hand shaking slightly.

Hine and Paul ate the rest of their food in silence and then went up on the top deck out at the front of the ferry. It was a beautiful evening and Hine took his hand again. The ferry rounded the end of Queens Wharf on its return run from Devonport and Calvert suddenly felt that all he wanted to do was pack up and leave this city. He had only been back from dreamland for a couple of days and already more things had happened to him in reality and paranoid imagining than happened in a year of dreams...*I remember I used to think as I sat by the railway - the railway of dreams...throwing stones on the tracks and looking at the rural road that was gradually returning, as we all do, to dust and dirt...how by that railway up on the cliffs, overlooking the sea of dreams...the number of cars in a year along that coast road would have equaled the number of cars in a day or less on any of Auckland's main roads...* now gliding into the wharf on the Kestrel with Hine on his arm, Calvert felt like that road of dreams if all the Auckland traffic had decided to descend upon that road built to hold nothing but dreams or nightmares - te moemoeä, te kuku anö.

This Tamaki Makaurau, this place of a thousand lovers, had been transformed into the place of a million fuckers all boogeying on down, all jostling and jiving for position, all moving and grooving, and the town and its people struggled under its magical weight. He had been back two days and he wanted to slip-slide back into that other time, that other world. But as he said to Hine, "I'm tired, let's go straight home!" Paul Calvert knew that he had got the last train out of the station of dreams! There was no going back from reality...*I got off the train at the junction and I was heading in the direction of a personal pilgrimage...the station was dark and cold, it was the middle of the night and there was no connecting bus for eight hours...it was the first time out of Auckland alone but I wasn't alone...Te Atua wanted me to reach the shrine to teach me nothing - the opposite of what I thought I already knew...on the journey to the junction the night sky had been like a glimpse of the unknown...snow-covered mountains stood against the sparkling jewels of stars and moon...I was now in the after midnight station wondering how to move...a goods train was pulling out in a few minutes and I jumped aboard the goods van...there was a coal-stove burning and the mixture of warmth and tiredness soon sent me to sleep...I awoke on the train in the railyards in the early morning rain, near the eye of Te Ika a Maui...it was raining heavily by the time I reached the outskirts of the town which was out on a limb...I drank a bottle of frozen milk and honey, then I was carried towards te Hiruhärama hou, half slouching, half conscious...at every bend in the river I woke with a start, it appeared we would all go off the edge at any moment...enticed all the way by the meandering mystery of Tutaeporuporu who followed in front of us...the shrunken head moved forward in time and place, te wä, te wä, you've given me your wah wah, and there were a thousand of them...turuturu mökai, and to the north and to the west a warning to those who choose to come here...you too might end up a steak with your head on a stake like a thousand others...but back to the river and the journey where the taniwha follows and plays with you...I remember the words of the dead one I have come to see 'and what has He to tell me? More stupid than a stone, what do you know of love? Can you carry the weight of my Passion, You old crab farmer. I go back home in peace'...after a few days pruning trees with Colin and seeing Deborah arrive porangi and a ward of the Priest, I too go back home in peace...I too know nothing of love...which in turn breaks my peace through the long short years of dreams...*When Hine and Paul arrived home at her house Hone was at home alone.

CHAPTER 2

"Kia Ora! You two look a bit happier now," Hone said. "I just had a kai, but there's still some pork bones in the pot if you hungry."

"We've just eaten thanks. What have you been up to all day, Golly?"

"Nothing much, apart from worrying about you two. I met Skids down at the Ponsonby pool-rooms and we had a few games. He's quite good for a young fella! Oh yeah, Paul, I ran into an old friend of yours who said he might have a room in his flat for you.

"Give him a ring, here's the number. Quite funny really, I remember him from when I first met you, eh, we all used to call him just 'The Third'".

"You mean you saw old Houston Eggars, really! I haven't seen him for about ten years. He and Blunt and I used to be inseparable in those days."

"Yeah!" said Golly with a wry smile on his face. "We, all the four of us used to drink up the Kiwi and then you'd all take me along to your honky-tonk university parties as a token black to show how liberal you all were."

"That's a bit unfair, old boy!" Calvert retorted in mock hurt. "Besides, I never knew you to turn down any of the drink that was so 'liberally' flowing."

"Oh! Shut up you two," said Hine, interrupting their well-worked banter. "Come and see this on the TV or let me see it in peace! Make a cup of tea at least, eh!" She said laughingly.

"I'll give old Eggars a call." Paul went to the telephone in the hall.

"Can I speak to Houston Eggars, please. How are you me old mate? Must be a long time since we spoke to each other. Yeah, Golly told me, where are you living? Way out in Manurewa. Oh well, I suppose beggars can't be choosers. Well, I'll stay here tonight and I'll get the bus out tomorrow. Is it far from the bus-stop? - OK, give me the address and I'll look it up on the map. What are you doing anyway Hous? - Yeah, OK we'll talk when I see you tomorrow. So, I get the One O'clock Papakura bus, look forward to seeing you, eh!"

"E Paul, come over here and sit beside me, this is quite good on TV." Then Hine called to Hone, "You made that cup of tea yet, eh mängere?"

"Well, it's all the way out in bloody Manurewa, but it's better than a poke in the eye with a sharp stick," Paul said...*in the Papakura shops I saw the blue Dinky convertible I think...I was off school for a day and me and my little brother went for a ride with dad ...as we drove along the Great South Road we could see all the big dump trucks and earth-moving machines cutting and levelling the ground all through South Auckland making the new motorways...they were even as far as Wiri, a place I'd never heard of before...we waited out in the back of our old van while dad nipped into the Jolly Farmer, just south of Papakura...every half hour or so dad would come out with a lemonade and sarsaparilla for us and he'd say 'I've just met so and so, I'll only be five minutes'...then off he'd go back into the pub leaving behind our cries of 'Aw Dad, why can't we come in' and 'Give us a bob for a hot pie'...this last piece of semantics used to leave my brother and I in hysterics...'Give us a bob,' he'd say. 'What for?' I replied. 'Give us a bob for a hot pie!' and we'd be away laughing our heads off like a couple of imbeciles...as we* were going back through Papakura on our way home to Orakei, I cried out as we passed the toy shop, 'Stop! You promised to get me that convertible, dad, you promised!'...'Oh, all bloody right! Here's ten shilling, and bring the bloody change back,' he said good-humouredly. 'Thanks, dad'..."Thanks Golly," Paul said as Hone handed him a cup of tea.

It was Saturday night, but Hine and Paul went to bed early after Golly had left to go to a party.

"See you at work on Monday, eh bro," he said as he walked out the door. He added, "You know where to go, eh, to the yard in Mt. Eden, just off View Road. Be there about 7.30, eh! See you. Bye sis!" Hine and Paul just lay quietly in each other's arms, talking softly and joking to each other. She suddenly went funny and said,

"Paul. I'm afraid of being alone, but I'm also afraid of being with someone, you especially."

Calvert wasn't ready for this, but he was tired and didn't really feel like a big heart to heart discussion or any kind of argument.

"Why?" he asked, somewhat diffidently.

"Oh! I don't know, it's all been too quick. Like, I mean you only arrived back in Auckland a few days ago, I hadn't seen you for a long time and now we're lovers, and all this camera and Mercedes, Nazi business, well you know!"

He stroked her hair gently, we were silent for a while, then he said,

"I know it's difficult, Hine I'm just as confused as you are, probably more, because I've got to find out about all this nonsense. I have to re-evaluate my whole life. As I said to Tony, while this answers a few questions about my life, it brings out a great many more to answer. My bloody father might have been one of those fucking mass-murderers that you read about, and what's more he might even be alive." Here he paused for a moment, then continued, "And even my presumptive father may have been an I.R.A. gunman, although I feel a lot closer to that cause than I could ever feel about bloody Nazis. Jesus! And now I have to think that my own bloody mother who I trusted and loved all through my childhood and her death, now I have to think that even she was lying to me all those years."

Paul was almost yelling by this time in a rage of incomprehension. He'd all but forgotten where he was as he let out all the pain and confusion that had been inside him the last couple of days.

"Hine, I just don't know any more"...it's like knowing nothing in te wahi kuku, te täone nui köhatu, the city of stone and the landscape of dreams, te whenua moemoeä, where the stone age people, he tangata porangi, lived out their mad fantasies...no one knew anything here, everyone had been framed...even the Disney castle had cracks in it, not just the people...[the picture] one who walked here saw the yellow peril destroying the White man's world and murdered a Chinese man (Paul Sherriffs No.9, No.9, No.9, Revolution – and they say it is a capital offence)...but now everything is over-grown and the buildings are like world war ruins...a truck moved through the smouldering bricks and the woman in black, my lover, walks like a widow at sunset in dreamland...it is a mild, beautiful southern evening and there I am on the lance-corporal's truck as we move away *from this demolished building, te whare kuku, te whare porangi where nightmares no longer haunt the sleepless days...out of these ashes the phoenix of the moon will rise over the sea just seen through the flowering magnolia...you could hear the mournful sound of the 5.30 container train moving up into and towards the oncoming night...a single light and a single sound moving through the pathways of the past...the old Mäori tracks along the coast were overlaid by rails in the late half of the last century by Chinese labourers...*"Oh, Hine," Paul cried, "I feel like I don't know anything any more. All my education and knowledge and books have taught me nothing, it seems, at a time like this. Most of all about you. Hine, I hesitate to tell you I love you and I realise you have every right to be suspicious of that kind of thing, well, I just don't know. Of course I share your distrust of 'relationships' and I know the pitfalls..."

"Paul, just be quiet, eh."

"I'm sorry but . . ."

"Just be quiet Paul," she repeated gently. "I don't want to hear any more about anything!" Hine turned out the bedside lamp and they both lay there in the darkness. Paul felt uncomfortable and unsure about what he should do. He thought what a bloody idiot he must have seemed raving on like that but he daren't say any more to Hine until she had said something. After a while he heard her fumbling with the radio-cassette player next to her lamp and then came the soothing, funky, banal beat of reggae music.Hine seemed happier and she turned towards him and said softly,

"Hold me close, Paul."

Taking this somewhat prematurely as an indication that she wanted to make love he made a few familiar motions, but she said

"No, Paul, not now, not tonight. Just hold me in your arms and we go to sleep, eh."

And suddenly he felt exhausted and slowly drifted towards *te wahi moemoeä* in a *waka* made of Hine's body and the music: 'Is this love, is this love, is this love that I'm feeling?' Bob 'Marley and Paul Calvert made up Hine's canoe...*haere ki te moe...how often did I dream of the reality of Tania when I was in dreamland...she was always in my thoughts, my feelings were all for her, but she was never in my arms...'is this love'...and then...deeper down into te wahi kuku...here is where the dark spirits live and I betrayed a whole roomful of people to save the life of my friend Richard...'Unfortunately there is no such thing as rehabilitation of the blood' said Obergruppenfurher Gala Day as he pushed the battered body of Richard to the floor. A smile came to his cruel, handsome face as he turned to me and said, 'You have done well. The Reich salutes you'...and he handed me thirty pieces of silver. Then he ordered his men to shoot the people I had betrayed in front of me. 'You will, of course, join me for supper, Herr Calvert'...in dreamland I had awoken from my nightmare with Tania beside me in bed...she was awake in her living nightmare...'Hold me tight, don't let me go!'...her drugs were inside her pushing nightmares through her body into her soul ...I held her and she clung to me, her body twisted around mine like a plant climbing its way around a tree...the beautiful melancholy of despair infused itself from her anguish into my veins and we were one...but love got in the way and* *destroyed the beauty of closeness...in dreams and in reality I followed her but she had already caught the scent of fear on the wind and was off, te whatinga moemoeä o te ätaahua...so I live in an empty dreamland where the mist rolls onto the hills early in the day and the moon appears mournful and solitary in the ever-darkening sky...*Hine was shaking him, "Get up! Get up! It's nearly midday. You better hurry if you wanna get the bus at one." She gave me a cup of tea and eggs on toast.

"Eat this quick!" she said.

Paul nearly said something about her wanting to get rid of him, but then remembered that things were a bit delicate between them and elected to say only,

"Kapai te kai, e wahine ätaahua."

She smiled at him and left the room. Calvert ate his breakfast, got dressed and kissed Hine good-bye. She was sitting down watching the beginning of the Sunday afternoon movie on TV. As he was leaving he turned to Hine and said,

"Oh, by the way madam, I have an invitation to dine with the esteemed Tony Blunt and his lady wife tomorrow night. I wonder, if it's not being rather forward, if you, madam, should like to join me as my dining companion?"

Hine looked at him and laughed, saying "Me, go to those posh honkie's place, you joking. I wouldn't know what to say, eh!"

Paul pretended to be offended, so then she said, "OK, I'll meet you at the pub after work and we'll talk about it, now push off, can't you see I'm watching the TV."

As he walked to the Three Lamps intersection Calvert could see a bus approaching so he ran to the bus-stop by the Ponsonby shops. The bus had as its destination 'Downtown Auckland.' He got to the Municipal bus depot with about ten minutes to spare, so he went and sat in the waiting room. This was always a place of intrigue and mystery to him as a child, as well as a regular haunt. He was fascinated by the wood paneling, its light brown varnish that was now partially covered by murals, at once welcoming and aloof. He remembered how his mother and the girls would disappear behind the sign 'LADIES' and he'd sit and wait. It used to be so quiet except for a few people talking, but nowadays there were kids with their ghetto-blasters blaring out the rueful reggae beat Rastaman vibration, positive-live as you wanna live, someone playing a battered old guitar with a few others singing, some bewildered older Päkehä people wondering 'what's be happen', their lives had been permeated by a 'live as you don't want to, but as you should!' philosophy. As Paul Calvert looked around the various signs and destinations he see that the Orakei bus platform has been changed...*the Orakei bus, having turned into Ngaiwi Street from Ngapipi Road grinds its way up towards the Coates Avenue shops...as the old green Daimler ascends the hill, I am a somewhat indolent twelve year old heading home after being in town for the morning...a new fare section begins at the shops where I paid to get off but the next stop along is where the track going down to my house in Tautari Street begins...I decide to risk it and override rather than pay the extra 2d...everything is all right until it comes time for me to get off...'Open the back door please driver' I say for the second time but I realise my attempt to defraud* the A.T.B. has been foiled...'I'm sorry, driver, I must have been dreaming and gone past my stop'...'No, I haven't got any money left, I spent it on an ice cream'...'Get off! And if I catch you doing this again, I'll get the police. You Orakei Bastards are all the same!'...when I first got off the bus I felt good but then I saw one of our family friends had been on the bus and I felt ashamed and I was scared she would tell mum..."Hey, man, cat over there said give you this." A tall, young Polynesian towered over where Calvert sat.

"What, cat?" Paul Calvert said, only slowly breaking out of his reverie. "Who are you?"

"I's just standing over there by Gore Street and this dude pulls up in a big black car sayin' to me and point'n to you 'give this to him!' and he give me this note for you, and this note for me!"

He held out both his hands, one at a time in two 'gimme five' gestures. In his right hand he had a fifty dollar note and in his left hand was a piece of paper folded in two. The letter he handed to Calvert and then he started to walk away. Paul Calvert was about to run after him but noticed the time was almost One O'clock. Running out of the waiting room he leapt on the Papakura Railways bus.

"Manurewa please!"

Paul sat down in the virtually empty vehicle and opened the note: it read, 'Don't forget your heritage, you are a white Protestant male.' It had a picture of three wise monkeys, each wearing swastika arm bands, and they were saying 'Hear no evil, See no evil, Speak no evil.' At the bottom of the page was a little sachet of white powder beside which were the words 'If you don't stop going with that black slut you will be arrested by the police for selling Heroin. Remember, you are no longer in dreamland'...in dreamland, te wahi moemoeä, moemoeä, Tania and I were at the pub one night, - her daughter was staying at Aunty Win's...Tania and I had been to dinner and were enjoying each other's company...this was all before I told her I loved her against my instincts and everything collapsed...Tania had gone downstairs to get some cigarettes and I was standing at the bar talking and drinking with a chap called James...he was working on a fishing boat out of Port and I had seen him now and then and always enjoyed his company...suddenly, 'Kuku'...he said, 'I saw you talking to that black bitch, Tania, you should keep away from them, her in particular. She really fucked-up a good friend of mine, you know him, and'...but I was no longer listening, I was confused and angry, I wanted to punch him, to knock him to the floor, to boot him - anything - Tania, Rangi, Golly, Wini, all my Mäori friends flashed through my mind, all the ones who had taught me so much just by being there...yet, I could not respond violently, so my emotions turned inward and I felt physically ill...'Where you going, Paul?' called James, 'stay and have another drink'...but I was away...I went looking for Tania, but I was only dreaming then - kei te moemoeä au..."Remember, you are no longer in dreamland" Calvert said to himself.

As the bus, with its traditional suburban dull metallic blue and white livery of NZR Road Services, moved down Khyber Pass and into Newmarket, Paul Calvert re-read and re-read the note. It was obvious what it was about and who it was addressed to. But, who had sent it and why? As the bus turned into

Broadway he became confused and frightened, not just for himself but for Hine too! He never remembered the Great South Road being so long.

In dreamland long roads were short compared with those in Auckland. Every mile now travelled seemed to punctuate his dilemma and despair. Every significant junction or major town reminded him of a nostalgia for the past which only made his present predicament more unbearable. So as the bus trundled through this lazy Sunday afternoon, through Market Road shops, through Greenlane and Harp of Erin, through Penrose and across the rail overbridge, on towards Otahuhu he felt more and more helpless. Paul Calvert was thinking, almost dreaming...'I am moving through a past which is present towards a future which is an unfamiliar land of the past...I think how far away Ponsonby is, how far away from Hine, how can I warn her she may be in danger?...Who is doing this to us?...Is there a connection between these events and my father?   ...I just don't know!'...Papatoetoe, old daddy two-shoes where the toetoe grows high passes the bus window like a dream...it started raining, one of those heavy drenching downpours which deluge Auckland every now and then...as we drive up the hill of the chief's puku in te wahi moemoeä and look down to the right, the port of dreamland and the papiermache peninsula look like toyland...we are flying – la, lala la lala la, as we have a smoke and somebody spoke and echoed the dream...as the road twists and turns, the Chev is like a B29 bomber flying in low over a European landscape...snow begins to fall and our mission begins to falter...it is coming down heavily and roads ice over under the white covering...we lose contact with base as we go into a nose-dive...the white land, the chief is wearing his white feather cloak today, waiting for a special guest, and here we are like ants crawling over his belly, trying to escape after he's had a good scratch...the Chev slides sideways at a corner and we are stuck, blocking off the road ...it's only a dream and we get out laughing and throw handfuls of snow as the traffic banks up either side of us...each time the car moves, it moves towards the edge of the hill until the only thing that stops it rolling down is a farmer's fence post...it is getting dark when we finally, on our last attempt and with a little help from our friends, get the old crate back on her flight-path, which is now homeward bound...we have abandoned our haerenga ki Parimoana and as the snow deepens around us we are happy to be getting out of it...coming into Manurewa, Calvert tells the floating bird of dreams to be off - Atu! Atu! He manu moemoeä, haere atu! 'How can I dare dream at a time like this?' he thinks to himself.

The rain, te ua nui, is coming down as the bus pulls into the stop! Feeling miserable and confused Paul runs for the bus shelter as the bus moves away, south, to the edge of dreamland. Suddenly, as he tries to find his street map, he notices a large black car come racing round the corner. He can think of only one thing, and flings himself to the ground in the hope that they haven't seen him.

Lying still on the wet, cold concrete from under the bus stop he can see the wheels of the car which has now slowed to a crawl. The car stops just outside the covered end of the shelter and Paul sees the doors open and just there in front of his nose are two pairs of large, black boots standing outside the car. He is trying not to make a sound or a movement.

"I wonder where he went to. I was sure I saw someone get off that bus as we came over the rail-bridge" one of the men said. Just at that moment, despite his fear, the damp got the better of Calvert and he sneezed loudly. He leapt up and prepared to run for his life, half feverish from paranoia and the cold, when he heard a voice call,

"Calvert! You stupid bastard, what were you doing lying on the ground?" Paul looked around and there was Houston Eggars 'The Third', and one of his friends.

"We come to pick you up in our Māori Limousine and all you can do is lie on the ground, hiding from us and catching a cold into the bargain, thus defeating our purpose of preventing you getting wet! What a - how do you say it Rewi?"

"Porangi" said a great big Māori fellow, who stood next to Houston, wearing a green Swandri and great big leather riding boots, and a smile right across his face.

"Yes, that's it, porangi!" said Eggars.

Paul Calvert looked over towards what he had thought was a sinister late model Mercedes Benz to find that the black beast that had come screeching around the corner, and had made me hit the deck, was in fact a slightly battered black Mark II Zephyr. At the sight of this he went into fits of laughter, almost falling over at the absurdity of his own folly, and the world became quite weird and wonderful to him after all the anxiety and fear that he had recently experienced...*the dreamland Mark II moved like a rocket through central dreamland craters and lunar-type rock formations...also, like a rocket, it used as much oil as it did petrol...long straight roads and then into the ancient river-gouged gorge...this was a previous attempt I had made to leave te wahi moemoeā but as I found out, leaving dreams wasn't that easy...the tug of the heart...kumekume o te manawa...the artist with his Harris Tweed and a loaded rifle, future Fitz of laughter, rain and tears, and the dreaming rain-a-pouring down as the trio trekkarred through* the *non-windscreen wiper central night...I drivin' in the holy virgin rain, just a jeepster they passed the whiskey rounds a-live a-live-o...*as they pulled into Eggar's driveway Paul caught a glimpse of his new home. He had been telling Houston and Rewi the events which had led to his peculiar behaviour at the bus stop.

As Calvert told his story Rewi had punctuated the more ludicrous junctures, exclaiming, "Is that so old boy?" in a mock upper-class accent. The house where they lived was a 1940's or 1950's State house nestled amongst several dozen similar edifices. Eggar's sister, Elizabeth, had married Rewi after several years knocking around with him. Originally, they had settled up in the North on some land belonging to Rewi's iwi, but both had decided to come the big smoke when Rewi lost his job at the local freezing works. Now Elizabeth was pregnant with their third child, and the same fate of a freezing works closure meant that Rewi was out of a job again, only this time in the city!

"Hello Liz!" Paul said and gave her a kiss. "Long time since I've seen you eh dear. I hear you've got another bun in the oven."

"It feels like a bloody Christmas cake this time!"

"More like chocolate cake eh!" said Rewi, smiling.

Paul suddenly thought about Hine and felt a pang of anxiety about her safety.

"Where's the phone, Houston, please?" Eggars pointed to the hallway. Calvert picked up the receiver and dialled the number.

"Kia Ora!" He heard Golly's voice. "Hone, is Hine there? You don't know where she is? Okay, ask her to ring me at Eggars' as soon as she gets in. Have a good night last night? - really! Kapai, eh! See you at work in the morning, and don't forget to tell that sister of yours to ring me"...*'I don't know what to say' comes her minimal reply...'How are you?' 'Alright.' 'How's Melissa?' 'Alright, she wants to see you.' 'But you don't?' 'Was telling you I love you that bad'...'Your three minutes is up, sir, if you wish to continue this call have your money ready' then Tania's voice 'I'll see you when you come to town' then the click of her hanging up, then silence...I can think of nothing but Tania as I walk down the railway line...I look behind the dreamvillage, past the cliffs to the sea, where the early afternoon fog is beginning to roll onto the land...soon the whole area will be covered by a grey blanket and then my thoughts and feelings will be reflected in nature's melancholy...te parimoana o taku manawa, te kohu o taku wairua...*"You two kids, go and say hello to Uncle Paul and then get ready for your baths!" Elizabeth's voice told you that she loved her children, you could hear that indulgent, protective tone even in the most pedestrian of her phrases when she spoke to them.

They were both beautiful children, and as in a lot of half Māori half Pākehā people, the best of both races are often featured in the children... *I remembered telling Melissa that she was lucky to have both the bloods of our country because she would realise the richness of feeling and thought people who took the trouble to explore both aspects of Aotearoa New Zealand and would be well rewarded...I knew that this was a bit above a child's understanding...but when Tania had told me how she'd come home from school saying "Mum, I don't want to be a Māori" I thought that if I instilled in her a good feeling about her mana it might counteract what was happening at school..."Why do they always beat me up 'cos I'm the only white boy in the class"..."I don't know Jimmy," says Frank as he and I sat in his Ponsonby house, playing a game of chess.."You get a glass of milk and go outside and play, Paul and I are playing chess."..."It's becoming a bit of a worry, this business with Jimmy, Paul. The other night he came home quite hurt and he had 'honki' written all over his school bag...I know you feel sympathetic to these Maoris, but"...I could feel an argument coming on, so I just told him about Melissa and he became quite quiet..."It's funny how this kind of thing can happen so differently in two Ponsonby schools: Your move," said Frank...*"Hello, Uncle Paul." "Hello Unca Porl." The smaller child's voice echoed her older brother's, and they both ran off giggling and fighting towards the bathroom.

Elizabeth and Paul were alone in the kitchen, Eggars and Rewi having gone outside to chop some firewood and bring it in. Liz and Paul Calvert had been quite good friends when he was going to University with her older brother, they even went out together for a while.

"Want a cup of tea, Paul?" He said he'd love one and then said,
"How's things, Liz?"
She stood at the bench, her hands being warmed by the tea cosy on the pot.

"It's been hard lately. Since Rewi lost his job I mean. He hates being on the dole, thinks of himself as a bludger. He went out and got drunk one night a couple of weeks after he'd been laid off. He's not normally a drinker, but this night he was. He came home right off his head and he laid into me! It was terrible Paul. First his words and then his fists. I was screaming and woke the kids and of course that set them off - it was like a mad house! Eventually he just started crying, and then he crashed on the floor. It was like a great tree falling - not just physically.

"The next morning he thought I was lying when I told him what he had done. But when I showed him the cuts and bruises and when the children wouldn't go near him he was forced to believe it. He hasn't touched a drop since, and I'm pretty sure he won't. But sometimes I look at him and I can see the anger and despair in his eyes and it really frightens me. His whole mana came from the fact that he was the bread-winner, the provider of his family. Now he feels less than useless."

Calvert was just about to say something when Rewi walked in with an armful of wood in one hand and an axe in the other. He was a big, powerful man and Calvert couldn't help thinking how defenceless Liz must have felt that night.

"How about a cup of tea for the workers, e Liz," said Rewi.

"It's already made, dear!" she replied.

"Did you show Paul his room, eh Liz?" said Rewi.

"Oh that's right: come here Paul" said Elizabeth, "you pour the tea Rewi, thanks."

The room that Elizabeth showed Paul to was something like a sun-porch in size but a lot darker. It had a single bed and a small wardrobe for furniture. Had there been anything else it would have been over-furnished. There was a small window at the far end of the room which looked out onto a concrete driveway, a fence and then a similar house to this one.

"It's a bit small, I know, but at least it's somewhere for you to stay until you get on your feet"...*parimoana i roto i te wahi moemoeä...through the window of my little house I could watch the sun rising over the horizon of the sea...the land and the trees and the sky would shine with the touch of the golden rays...the sun shone, not on the nothing new, but transforming the morning and thus making everything new...the fragrance of the flowers, the call of the birds, every now and then old 'one-leg,' the local hawk, would fly by*...suddenly, out of the corner of his eye, Calvert could see a cop-car pulling up outside the concrete driveway. He pushed Liz out of the way and ran out into the living room, nearly knocking one of the children over. He grabbed his jacket and fumbled through the pockets until he felt in his hand the small sachet of white powder attached to the note he had been given at the bus terminal.

Fortunately, Rewi had got the fire going and the first flames were beginning to leap towards the chimney. At the moment the cops came bursting in Calvert threw the note and the plastic bag onto the fire, hoping they would be well alight before the boys in blue noticed it. Things got a bit crazy and the cops were as much taken aback as any one else. Liz had come running out from the room ready to get stuck into Paul for being so rough. However, when she saw the police she must have done a bit of quick arithmetic and began berating them for coming into her house, upsetting her children who by now were both crying and screaming their heads off. She demanded to know on what pretext they had entered her premises.

"What has my husband done wrong?" she screeched at them and Paul noticed the younger of the two men in uniform visibly recoil from the lioness protecting her family.

"It's not your husband that we are after, Mrs Watene," said the senior policeman, being as conciliatory as possible. "We have reason to believe that there is a Mr. Paul Calvert staying with you and that he may be in possession of hard drugs."

As the sergeant said this Calvert was watching the last semblance of the evidence against him melting into oblivion of heat and flames and it was with some relief that he could answer the cop's question to him about whether this was true.

"No!" was his indignant reply.

The younger cop was ordered to search him and his belongings. He did this somewhat over-vigorously, having regained some of his reassurance and arrogance after being made vulnerable by Elizabeth's tirade.

His task was not made easier by the fact that the little three year old Tahana kept going up to him, hitting on the back of his legs, saying 'leave unca Pori alone!' and then running back to her mummy. Curiously, the older cop let this go unchecked, and after a short while said,

"Come on Johnson, if you haven't found anything by now, you won't be likely to! Do you mind showing us your bedroom Calvert?"

On the way out of the room the older cop stopped and looked into the fire, for what seemed like an age. Calvert could feel the fear and anxiety building inside him. What could he see? Was there a smell he recognised as heroin being burned? Was there still a part of the note that hadn't yet burned? He was beginning to sweat as the cop turned to him and said,

"Mmmmm, you can't beat a good hot fire, no matter what they say about all these new-fangled inventions. I grew up in Otago, and down there a fire and a coal-range are part of life. Look at you, Calvert, sweating like a pig. Good to see a man sweating after a good chop at the wood," he winked at Paul, knowingly or unknowingly he wasn't sure, and then they went to his room...*I remember the cops came round the side of the house in Orakei...'No, no he's not here' said my mother...when the bluebeats had left, mum took me and my brother into the kitchen, our sisters were younger and sleeping...'You two boys are old enough to know,'...mum was trying not to cry, 'dad's got to, he's got to go to jail,' at that word mum started to cry...my brother and I looked at each other and almost burst out laughing, our usual response to bad news...but we saw mum was still upset so we both looked away from each other and tried to make mum feel better...the next day a friend came over and took us all to Whitianga, except dad...dad arrived a couple of days later...it was a wet night and when he told us he had got a taxi from Auckland it was like a magical event...*"Well, Johnson," Inspector Wilkinson said at length, "doesn't seem to be anything here! My advice to you,

Calvert, is keep your nose clean. I think there's something going on around here, and we'll be keeping an eye on you. We don't normally get an urgent tip-off about a big drugs dealer on a Sunday afternoon and I'd like to tell you now that you are definitely under suspicion, even though we can't pin anything on you. Damn shame you forgot to trace that call, Johnson."

The inspector and his side-kick were just about out the door. Johnson striding arrogantly ahead seemed to have an odd, knowing look in his eye. The older policeman turned to Calvert. In a low voice, with Johnson deliberately or so it seemed, out of ear-shot, he said,

"Keep this to yourself Calvert . I don't know what's going on but there's a few things about this affair which strike me as being a bit odd. Call me during the week if you think there's anything you can tell me."

Then in a loud voice, he said, "You heed this warning, Calvert, or else you're in big trouble!"

"What's going on!!!" Elizabeth's 'hell hath no fury' voice, distraught and accusing, met Calvert as he went back into the living-room. Rewi and Eggars, who already knew about the dope being planted on me, were quick to his rescue, explaining what he had told them.

"You should have told me when you first came in, all of you are to blame. I know all about the lack of time, how you forgot because it was nice to see me and all that, but you still should have told me. Rewi, you know you should have told me." Liz glared at her husband, then continued,

"I thought they'd come to take my husband from me. I always remember reading Baxter about the crimes of having long hair, having no jobs and above all, being Mäori. In those days it was just a book I read at University, but of course it's all come a lot closer to home, especially since Rewi lost his job. It's about time you men grew up, it's no game! Look at my darling babies crying their little hearts out because they're frightened. Come here babies, it's alright, come to mummy." The children came over to their mother, bewildered and uncertain. Liz held the close and continued,

"I don't mind you staying here Paul," she turned and faced him, at once furious and yet kind, "but you must realise I've got other lives to look after now. I've got a family under pressure - and now, because of some weird bloody Nazi drug dealers - Nazi! Oh! for Christ's sake!"

At this Liz gave out a kind of laugh of disbelief, and then said to her children,

"Come on my darlings, come with mummy and lie down and I'll tell you both a story, and everything's going to be alright!"

Elizabeth and her two children, who were still sniffling and weeping quietly went off into the bedroom leaving three embarrassed men looking into the fire. Paul was particularly shattered and for some time felt just pure pain and mental anguish. He wanted to leave Auckland at once, a kind of knee-jerk reaction that would have him back in dreamland safe and secure in the failures and nightmares of yesterday rather than facing the reality of his present situation. It was starting to get dark but still the unholy trinity sat, none of them able to move for fear that the world might fall apart.

Eventually, the silence was broken by the sound of the children laughing in the other room, and Rewi somewhat reluctantly said,

"I'd better go and see them, eh!"

Eggars and Calvert just sat as the night descended, the fire gradually dying but their emotional indolence was stronger than any desire for warmth or comfort...*the lights of a barely audible mantle radio came from one side of the room...my mother came into the room, I was listening to the radio in the kitchen...the light was out and I was enjoying the music, looking at the dial that was lit up and had the names of famous cities, New York, Paris, Sydney, London...'You shouldn't listen to the radio in the dark dear, only queers do that!'...she turned on the light and I felt angry and confused and dazed by the bright light...'What do you mean, mum?' I asked. 'Homosexuals like things to the dark, like listening to the radio, you'll understand when you grow up'...there have been many things I've never got to understand by growing up, and this is one of them...still, your mother's your mother for all that, and even with the light on I'm still aware of the darkness within which never leaves...*the phone rang and Eggars got up and walked indifferently to answer it in the hall.

"It's for you, Paul."

Suddenly, he remembered that Hine was meant to ring. What could he tell her about this latest outrage. It was her, and they talked about a few superficial things. It seems that she was alright. She'd spent day with a friend in the Domain. He didn't want to upset her, so he just made the arrangements for going to the Blunt's the next day, and left it at that.

It was dark and Eggars and Calvert decided to go for a walk to the shops and get some takeaways for the family for tea. The rain had cleared and it was a nice suburban evening. The streets were deserted and they walked slowly as he related to Eggars the bizarre story and events of the last few days. After a while Eggars interrupted.

"Well, I'm afraid Paul all I'm going to do is complicate things for you. My father, I don't think you ever met him, was out here from England a year or two. He's spent his life in the British Foreign Affairs and when he retired he decided to come and visit his itinerant prodigals in the antipodes. One night, Elizabeth and I were talking to him about our various New Zealand friends and in the course of the conversation, your name was mentioned."

Eggars paused as they came to the railway overbridge and stood and watched the southbound Northerner thunder underneath them. Paul Calvert felt like just jumping on the train's roof, like in the old cowboy movies, and riding all the way back to dreamland. He was almost dreaming when Eggars said, "Anyway, Father said, 'Oh! I knew a chap Calvert once, a right rascal he was too. Got us diplomats into all sorts of bother in Berlin before the war. Kept flirting with the Nazis - he knew some of the bigwigs in the Party. Roy Calvert! Yes, that was his name.' Of course," Eggars continued, "I had heard of your Uncle Roy, and so I told my father about your father. 'Load of nonsense, Calvert never had a brother called Richard.' He said" and Paul laughed at his friend's mimicry of his father.

"My father was adamant." Eggars continued, "but then he did remember that there was some sort of scandal about this after Roy Calvert died. Apparently

Calvert went to Trinity College for some reason and met a chap O'Hanlon who was studying Gaelic linguistics as a cover for running guns for the I.R.A. They came to some arrangement that O'Hanlon would pose as Roy's brother when he went on business trips. When the war broke out Calvert went back to live in England and became a Lancaster bomber pilot, probably to ease his conscience for betraying his country my father reckoned."

Paul Calvert was stunned into silence for the second time in as many days. He didn't know what to think. Who was he? Who was his father? his mother? who was anybody? Maybe he had been dreaming all along and had completely lost touch with reality.

"Eight pieces of fish and three dollars chips" he heard Eggars say to the person at the shop, but now nothing seemed real. He remembered T.S. Eliot's grand phrase about people not being able to stand too much reality, but this was becoming ridiculous!

Too much reality leads to unreality. He thought maybe he'd been hearing things, maybe Eggars had just been talking about the weather, or the England-West Indies test series, or his girlfriend. Or perhaps he'd been rambling off his latest poems to Calvert who mistook his imagination for my reality.

Perhaps he wasn't saying a thing, just walking beside him like he is now, as they headed homeward and all the time Calvert had been hearing the voice, of ngä tangata porangi. The voice of those in the bin, friends who have been directed by these monologues of the mind, who have been driven insane by their own fears of life. But as he walked silently next to Eggars, the feel of hot chips in his hands, the wind blowing freshly in his face is a reminder...*not that long ago, maybe yesterday, but not the yesterday we know, I sat on a large rock that looked like a head...it was a Manukau Head and I was at Whatipu during one of my returns from ngä moemoeä...I sat on this rock tablet, then twenty people and I looked down at sand and sea...thoughts and memories of Rangi and Tania washed over me like the waves on the rocks below me...the rock cradled my back and the incline of my head perfectly, so that I became the rock in reality while wave after wave of memory from dreamland washed over me, eroding and reshaping my form...from the air, te wairua o Te Atua, the wind, touched me, fresh and vigorous and I realised as each thought of Rangi, as each memory of Tania, as each element of the spiritual wind buffeted my crag-like face, I realised that this was love; the love of women and the love of God were testing me...like the wind and like the wave, love in the hard elemental fact of existence...always eroding and shaping life...if you're a coward you'll become a cave, hidden and hollow, as you hide from the elements of reality...if you're prepared to stand up and enjoy these winds and driving rains, baking sunshine and battering waves then you will live your life until the last pebble of your existence has eroded and you return to the life from which you came...I left Whatipu with the car stereo blaring and with an understanding I could take with me to dreamland and to the grave...*when Houston and Calvert got back they found Rewi and Liz and the kids in the living room. They were all laughing at something that was on their old, somewhat battered black and white box.

"Kapai te kai!" said Rewi, "I'll make us a Ti, eh!"

Paul Calvert felt extraordinarily tired, and even though there was a good Sunday night play on after 'Radio with Pictures' he went to bed. Everything was a lot more relaxed with Liz now, and as he said,

"Haere ki te moe, au," she came up to him and gave him kiss on the forehead. He heard Rewi say to Houston,

"Always make me laugh, eh, when I hear Pakehas speaking Māori. More Pakehas than Maoris speak it in the city now I think." Then Rewi said to Calvert,

"Paul! I got to go over to Otara in the morning to see about some job over that way, so I'll drop you at the station, eh!" Calvert said thanks and another goodnight to everyone then off he went to bed, wanting to have an early night so that he would be fresh and feel reasonably fit for work the next morning. He hadn't done a labouring job for a while, although it was the line of work he was most familiar with and quite good at. He turned the light off and for a short time was beginning to drift off. But a car driving past reminded him he was still alive and he suddenly went into a state of anxiety so acute that the more he tried to sleep the more wakeful he became. He was thinking anything that came into his head. Was he going mad? What was that look in the cop Johnson's eye? What did the three wise monkeys represent?

Of course now he'd thrown all the evidence on the fire, if he went around saying things like this to people, he'd be in Carrington before you could say BOO! Who was his father?, who was his mother? Was his real name O'Hanlon? Was his real father still alive and was there any connection between him and the people who had tried to set him up with the smack? This interesting speculation was one which he should have followed more than roughly if he hadn't at the same instant thought of Hine. Was she in trouble? Suddenly he felt helpless and worried about her. He needed her to be with him here in bed, to know that she was safe. But he also needed her here for selfish reasons. All he wanted was for her to come to him and with him, to take him away from the horror, the fears of his mind and of reality - for her to be physically, intimately close to him, to experience for those few moments of reassurance, of pure passion, the little death that helps us to forget mortality.

"It is impossible, it is absurd, but there it is! She is only solace against the darkness of existence." But then he thinks if she were here she must of course leave sometime and in leaving he would be more alone, even more helpless than before...*I am almost feverish. Exhausted, I fall into a fitful, restless sleep...te wahi kuku...te mate o taku wairua...I am alone in dreams...Rangi left and I am like a caged kahu, caught in my own prison ...every time I flap my wings I lose more feathers and bruise my body...in the cage of self the kahu had eaten it's own eyes for there was no other food...he had supped too often on the juice that the kereru loves, the crazy, deluding syrup that is too much for the austerity of the kahu...but I had done this to escape the reality of Rangi, the reality of dreams...*"Wake up, here's a cup of ti, we got ten minutes before we leave, eh!"

It was Rewi, and as Paul woke up and got ready for work he felt exhausted, as though he'd already done a days work. Rewi dropped him at Manurewa Station and Calvert told him he and Hine were going to the Blunt's for tea in the evening, so not to keep any kai. Also, he said he might not be home that night, he might stay at Hine's if she was in a good mood. Rewi laughed and then the Mark II roared off into the sunrise. Paul Calvert walked down onto the platform just as the train was pulling in. The familiar boom-cha-bom motion sent him to sleep and he only woke up at Newmarket when the call came over the station address system. "Newmarket Station, train to Auckland, Platform Two, passengers change here for Waitakere."

He suddenly remembered that he had to get to Mt. Eden. Grabbing his bag he leapt off just as the train began to move out. There was a five minute wait for the western train, so he just stood there feeling and, he thought, probably looking like a zombie!

The train rattled up the hill from Newmarket and under the Motorway, then stopped on the loop between Boston Road and Mt. Eden Prison. Calvert could hear the diesel engine murmuring away up front and looked out the window at the stone upon stone building which held the people who had stepped outside the law, inside! It was a reminder that anyone is capable of ending up on the wrong side of things - there but for fortune and all that.

A lot of debate goes on in Auckland newspaper columns about whether Mt. Eden Prison should be pulled down or transformed into a restaurant or some such thing, but Calvert couldn't help thinking it's good for people to have a reminder that things can go wrong in life. Not only to prevent such things happening to them, but also to remind them that there are many people languishing their lives away in one institution or another perhaps because others had not been a bit kinder and more understanding...*I went with my mother in the bus and we got off near Newmarket...we walked up Khyber Pass and along by the railway tracks...'Where are we going mum?'...'We're going to see dad, he's in this big prison that I told you about'...as we reached the large metal doors at the end of the avenue leading to the prison a man in a uniform and peaked cap opened a little peakhole and mum showed him some piece of paper...the man opened the door and let us inside...there were police everywhere and big bars and nets like we used to have to keep the chickens from flying away...there were about three or four stories of cells...and then dad came towards us...he looked grey and didn't have a moustache anymore, which made him really different...he briefly said hello to me and gave me a bit of a cuddle, and then he and mum went to one side and started talking secretly...the room we were in was like a big church hall and there were lots of people talking in huddles just like mum and dad...I was a bit bored so I wandered around for a while, then I met this young chap who wasn't talking to anyone..."What's your name?" he said to me..."Paul, what's yours?"...he said his name was Johnny and we started to have a conversation...we talked about pop music, and fishing, and planes and all sorts of things until mum came up..."Come and say good-bye to Dad"...again the familiar uneasy feelings that you have had about someone you've known all your life, but don't really know at all..."You be a good boy for your mother!"..."Yes dad"...and then we were out in the street...mum was crying and said, "They're moving dad to Wanganui. It will be nicer there for him but we won't be able to see him for a long time"...I nearly asked why but she was still upset so I left it..."I had a neat talk with that young man Johnny, while you were talking to dad"..."I know, I was* watching you. Johnny's in prison for murdering someone, Paul"...she must have seen a look of shock or something on my face for she added, "that doesn't mean you should think badly of him"...and I felt better because mum had said this kindly...as the train pulled out of the loop, the down train having gone through, so Paul's thoughts of Mt.Eden Prison receded and he braced himself for the day's labour ahead.

He got off the train and walked along Wynyard Road, towards the depot. There were dark clouds off towards the Waitakere Ranges, and rain was threatening. He hoped and almost prayed that the day would be rained out for he still felt drained from the lack of sleep and the events of the previous three days, including what amounted to quite a lot of drinking. Golly greeted him and introduced his friend to the boss and the gang.

They were mainly pre-release prisoners, and even the site boss, who was a bit of a character, had been inside for a few years for attacking someone from behind with a chain-saw when he was haurangi one time. His favourite saying was "I'm tough, but fair" and every time Calvert heard him say this he would think of him wielding a great bloody chainsaw and yelling out "I'm tough, but fair!" The site boss must have often wondered why Paul laughed for no apparent reason sometimes!

The rain held off until midday, despite the incantations by Rua of "Ua! Ua! Ua!" every time it started to spit. Rua was the gang's leading-hand and funny man. Anything that happened, or any time someone said or did something out of the ordinary, Rua was in with his quick wit and Calvert, being the new boy, took the brunt of his ngä kupuhauta all that morning...*te wahi moemoeä, te mahi o te rerewe...we were working up at Michie's Crossing repairing some broken sleepers after a derailment...there was a north-bound train due down any moment...our S9 gang were a funny looking lot, and I remember I used to compare them to the Hieronymus Bosch painting of Christ carrying the cross with a lot of weird, grotesque people all trying to ease the Saviour's load...I could pick out each character in the painting and give a name of one or the other of our railway gang to that character...I renamed the painting "Christ prepares to lay a sleeper at The Gums!" since the cross in Bosch's painting looked very like a railway sleeper, and there was a close resemblance between many of my fellow workers and the people in the actual painting...so there were Ted, Murch, Flook, Bob, Dave etc. all helping Christ to carry his cross up the hill to Calgary and there was Christ giving us all a hand to lay a sleeper after a derailment...while we waited for that train to come down the hill, it would be 160 - the first train north out of dreamland every morning - while we waited we all started talking while our shovels held us up...Flook curled up in a large concrete mixer and threw 'bon mots' into the conversation...Bob, who had a very sharp, sarcastic tongue picked up on the fact that I had been to university at one time. "So, old Pervert's (his name for Calvert!) been to Knob Hill. He didn't learn much did he, couldn't mix a good turd let alone a batch of concrete"...the conversation went back and forth and I had neither the wit nor the inclination to defend myself that day, having been drunk the night before...finally someone, Harry I think, said "What good are students for anyway?...at this Bob seized the moment and with an* uncharacteristic revolutionary allusion said, "They're quite good for target practice comrade"...everyone laughed and then someone yelled "Look out!" and old 160 pulled by a DJ locomotive thundered around the cutting corner, just missing at least two of us as usual..."You run out of concrete, eh, boy?" said Rua as Calvert realised he had been dreaming.

"You better wake up or else we think you working on the railway, like a sleeper maybe!" This mild dig plus his trip to dreams made Paul work twice as fast because that morning he could stand physical pain far more than he could any jibes or put down. The memory of Bob made him determined not to let Rua make him into some kind of laughing stock. He simply didn't reply to any taunts or provocations, just worked like a machine, so that although he felt exhausted in the extreme he felt no mental or emotional pressure.

At smoko Paul Calvert just sat quietly drinking a cup of tea, having the odd word with Golly in between hands of the game they were playing.

"Manila, this your round, you in?" Jim asked.

"No thanks, I'm a bit fucked and I've got no money till next week anyway."

"You won't have any money next week if you do play" said Rua, and everyone laughed. Paul was just about asleep when it was time to go back to work. The first thing he saw as he stepped outside the smoko hut was a black Mercedes. He felt confused and terrified, he'd forgotten all about that stuff after doing a good morning's work. The man who owned the Mercedes was a tall, handsome, well-dressed chap with blond hair and blue eyes. He was of fairly affluent appearance and acted as though he was born to rule. He was with our boss and they were both laughing and talking rather excitedly just out of earshot. Rua and the other boys gradually made their way out of the shed and to Calvert's surprise they all went straight towards the Mercedes.

"She's a beauty, e Den!" said Rua.

"Not bad eh, Rua. I picked her up this morning, only got here by ship on Saturday morning. It's not what you know, but who you know. My friend in Customs signed her release straight away!"

"Yeah man! I know what you mean, eh. My mate George, he stole the car I got on a Friday night, did the engine number and number plates and a quick paint job over the weekend and then I bought it off him on the Monday - pays to have friends O.K."

The strange man looked somewhat bemused and Rua turned and called to the workers "Haere atu ki te mahi! That means go back to work you lot for those who can't speak!"

"Who's that fella?" Paul asked Jim, as they walked over to get the concrete mixer going again.

"Oh, him, he's an old mate of the boss who made it good. He worked with our boss for many years in some kind of industrial spray company they set up together. I think he got sick of all the physical work and put his money into computers before they became widespread. Seems like he made the right choice! But our boss, he likes his work, I don't think he'd swap."

But Paul was hardly listening to Jim, he was too distraught at his own paranoia. The rest of the morning he went through the motions of mixing concrete. He ignored Rua's taunts about being a slow Päkehä, a useless bastard, and any number of other insults, with most of the others looking on, laughing. At one time he had to move a barrow full of concrete out of the way so he could get a fresh bag of cement. He lost his balance and both he and the barrow tipped over causing much mirth and a sharp rebuke from Rua. All this time, Golly was watching. He could see something was worrying his friend and he had a bit of verbal interchange with Rua about not picking on him. At last it began to rain.

"It's settling in I'd say, might as well go home" said the boss. On their way back to the depot they dropped Golly and Paul off at the Mt. Eden Station just in time to catch the midday train to Auckland. They got the bus straight from the railway to Ponsonby. When they got to Golly's they had a cup of tea and a bit of lunch. Then Paul had a shower and got into Hine's bed and went to sleep all afternoon...*te wahi moemoea, te wa o te huarahi mahi we were working on the roads and dreaming...the roads of dreamland just north of Parimoana wind and weave all along the eastern coastline...we were the road gang, our work ran parallel to the railway in place - but not in time...a few dream years or days before I had worked on the rail gang, now here on the same route roughly, I fix the roads not the rails ...the Boofer is in charge, he's only got one eye and he is one-eyed...no-one cares for the stupid old bastard who was put among us from another time...it is a relief for Beaconsfield and I to be put on the sewer-pipe job every so often where we laugh at the Aldo Moro Bar...but today we are bored, standing on a dusty road shoveling shingle...the Boof has gone to get another load of metal so the two us plus young Mike start acting the goat a bit, pick and shovel fights etc...one of the big dream-county trucks thunders along towards us...we recognise the driver so I pick up a shovel (being of Irish decent it would seem natural!) and throw it skidding along the ground...under the wheels of the big truck it goes, it snaps in two and the handle flies up in the air...the truck-driver gives us the fingers and drives off laughing...the Boof backs the truck back so that we can shovel the metal off it onto the existing pile...as I'm directing him and diverting his attention, Beaconsfield sneaks around and stealthily places the two broken bits of shovel under the back wheel   ..."Stop!" I shout, "you stupid old bastard, you just ran over the shovel". The Boof is rather surprised, "I've never done anything like that before in my life!"...I look over to my left and I see Mike and Beaconsfield fighting a losing battle to contain their laughter ..."Well, we can't do any shovelling without a shovel," I say in a deadpan fashion, trying not to make eye-contact with Beaconsfield, "you'll have to drive back to the depot and get us another shovel"...in a fit of rage he was out of sight in no time, the three of us collapsed into uncontrollable laughter!*...Golly woke Paul up with a cup of tea about four o'clock.

"Better get ready, e hoa, sis will be angry if you're late." Calvert felt a lot better after his moe, so he got dressed in the clothes he had brought with him. Skids came around and the three of them sat talking for ten minutes or so. Skids was telling the older men about his gang. Most of the areas which existed in the city centre were territorial apparently.

"Man, those trash in the city think they own it. We just go in from South on a Friday - we allowed in the city like anyone else - and then we get to the square they always tellin's us to fuck off and all that and then bang! you know----"

"See you later, Skids. Golly, I'll probably see you tonight, if I stay here, otherwise we'll get the train in the morning."

CHAPTER 3

Calvert had about half an hour before he had to meet Hine, so he decided to walk down College Hill instead of catching a bus. The rain had cleared and the sun, which was now low in the western sky, shone brightly. The footpaths were steaming as the ground warmed after the rain, and to the east, across Victoria Park, the hue of sunset had begun changing from turquoise to deep blue, and a streak of pink and mauve after-glow permeated through the tall buildings of Auckland's downtown area...*it was about eight o'clock on a Wednesday night and us kids were getting ready for bed...dad called us from outside, "Hey, come and see this!" mum complained that she had just got us all washed and it was too cold for us outside at that time...dad was adamant and so mum and us kids went out onto the front lawn...dad was talking to our next door neighbour and they were both looking out to where you just see the top of Rangitoto over Bastion Point from our Orakei house...at a time of night when normally the sky would have been black and the stars shining, the whole eastern skyline was lit up by a pink-orange glow..."the Yanks have let off another bomb in the Pacific," said dad...I stood there, I was about eleven years old, and I didn't know what to feel...it was exciting and beautiful, and yet I found I was strangely subdued..."How come you can see a bomb this far, dad?" "Boy, must be a big bomb!" said my brother, laughing...the girls were crying so mum took them inside, "Don't be too long you boys," she called to us*..."I'm glad you're here, I don't want to be here too long," said Hine as Paul walked into the bar. Then she said,

"You look nice. How'd your first day at work go, e!"

"It was alright. Tomorrow should be better, so long as Blunt doesn't get us drunk tonight!" Paul replied. Hine laughed and then got us a drink.

They left the pub and walked across Queen Street to catch the Benson Road bus outside the Civic. Hine began to get excited about having dinner with the Blunts. She was also a bit afraid.

"I never been anywhere in Remuera before."

Paul told her that Tony was a really nice chap, but that he too was a bit apprehensive about meeting Blunt's wife. Apparently she was from an English aristocratic family and could be quite snobbish.

"It'll be a bit of a laugh, especially if we get stuck into their booze!"

Hine looked at him.

"You already talking about getting haurangi, e, don't you remember what you said about ten minutes ago!" He looked at her, she was so beautiful. He suddenly put his arms around her, and kissed her gently on her long black hair and they sat in a loving embrace down the back seat of the Benson Road bus.

Calvert pressed the bell at the first stop after the Remuera Road shops and when they got off the bus they walked silently hand in hand. He could feel that they were close, perhaps in love with each other. The sky was now getting dark and reflected the feeling of deep blue melancholy and comfort which often accompanies moments of profound love. Walking slowly, savouring each minute of being with each other, their trance was only broken by Paul realising they had walked past Blunt's house. Turning around, Hine and Paul went back the way they had come and in a few moments stood at the front door.

"It's so quiet here, e!" said Hine. She was used to the hustle and bustle and close living of Ponsonby. In the Blunt's driveway, which was beautifully landscaped, there was a new Jaguar and a Mercedes sports car. The property was surrounded by a well kept hedge and the front gardens were dotted with rhododendron and rose bushes and featured a fountain, which was a statue of Bacchus.

The water went into the figurine through a wine goblet and came out through a certain lower aspect of this god's frontal anatomy. When Hine saw this she cracked-up laughing. "Looks like you!" she said, and Paul replied that while Bacchus' drinking cup did have a certain resemblance to the size of the vessel that he was used to imbibing from, he felt that the rather small appendage from which the god urinated bore no resemblance at all to himself and that he considered her words nothing less than an insult and he should prove her conclusively wrong later that evening. At which he picked Hine up and carried her towards the fountain. He was about to pretend to throw her into the surrounding pond when he heard Blunt's preposterous voice exclaim, "I say, Cara, do come and look at this, we've got a cave-man and cave-woman on our front lawn."

All this time Hine and Paul had been laughing and whooping out the Blunt's had been standing in the shadows of their verandah watching.

"We thought the peasants were mating, didn't we darling!" said Tony as his wife joined him.

Suddenly, Hine and Paul felt really stupid. He put her back on the ground gently and they both walked somewhat sheepishly back towards the house. Paul could tell

Hine was embarrassed and she started to apologise profusely. The Blunts just laughed, however, and Tony said he hadn't seen such goings on since Cambridge.

"But that was just between men, you understand," chuckling.

Cara said that her brother always used to pull similar pranks on her and the only reason she married Tony was – "to get away from the little swine. You realise he's thirty-three years old and still lives at home with Mummy and Daddy at Bochester Castle."

Still feeling somewhat subdued despite their host's reassurances, Hine and Paul sat down in the magnificent drawing room of the Blunts.

"Come in the Mercedes did you Calvert?" asked Tony, taunting him.

"Rather!" Paul said. "Got the chauffeur to take it back to the depot. He told me he'd be around about the same time as the last bus to pick us up, didn't he Hine?"

Hine just smiled and Tony asked what they wanted to drink. Hine and Paul looked at each other. They were both wondering if the sentiments expressed earlier about not drinking were stronger than their desire to drink. Finally Calvert said

"I'll have a small glass of water - with a large drop of whiskey in it!" and all four of them laughed. During dinner they all talked about nothing much rather vigorously. Tony seemed quite charmed by Hine and Paul enjoyed Cara's sophisticated banter and preposterous manners and habits. After an hour or two Blunt reminded them why we were there by saying,

"Oh, by the way Calvert, I've managed to dig up a few more bits and pieces in relation to that Nazi lineage of yours." Paul felt a little uneasy and reluctant to respond.

However, eventually he said, "Before we start on that I'd better tell you what's been going on with me!"

As Calvert began telling him about the dope incident with the note and the cops coming around to Eggars, he caught sight of Hine. She looked very strange, she'd gone very pale and before her tide of accusation poured out, he knew what he'd done wrong.

"Do go on," said Tony.

But Calvert said, "would you mind if Hine and I discuss something in private first?" "You fucking bastard, why didn't you tell me this first." Hine's torrent completely drowned out Blunt's reply of "No, of course not, old boy." Hine didn't stop to be polite.

Holding back tears, she laid into him, and he, being totally to blame for neglecting to tell her of the grubby little note calling her a 'black slut,' and involving her personally in what up to that point had been completely his own misfortune.

"For Christ's sake, Hine, I'm sorry. I forgot all about it this afternoon!" Calvert shouted at her. He was getting upset too by now.

"That's a poor fucking excuse, you dumb cunt!!! What you take me for eh, a bloody stupid Māori, or just a stupid woman - probably both, you bastard!" She screamed these words at the top of her voice and out of the corner of Paul's eye he could see Cara looking at Hine with a mixture of shock and bemusement, together with a kind of awe. In the situation she looked as all her delicate, well-bred English people do in the face of emotion. Calvert half expected her to come over to us and say something like, "Let's all have a nice cup of tea and forget about it, shall we?" This thought made him want to burst out laughing and it took an intense effort of concentration to return his attention to the tirade being delivered by Hine, who was by this time pounding him with her fists as well as her words!

Suddenly something snapped inside Calvert and he whacked Hine a beauty which sent her sprawling on the couch.

"Shut-up! - Just fucking shut up will you?" She went quiet as she curled up like a coiled snake on the couch. There was silence and Paul felt his blood and emotions boiling. He realised he was wrong - wrong not to have told her on the Sunday night, and wrong to have hit her. He'd never done such a thing before and he was trembling with self-disgust as well as all the other emotions of the moment. Tony and Cara had moved closer together and they both looked completely stunned by what was going on. It was Paul's duty to speak, to say something that could bring the situation back to normal. He looked at Hine who

Because of one stupid, ridiculous action he had split asunder the affection and trust between himself and Hine. That one incident, more than any of the stupid I.R.A. and Nazi stuff, had upset the whole evening. It was completely his own doing and now he had to pay for this gross behaviour by the rift it had caused in his relationship with Hine, since she was not willing to forget...*Tania lay in my arms sleeping...it was the last time we were together i roto i te wahi...and now it haunts me this time, this time of closeness and harmony when male and female elements are united...as Tania lay in my arms I was thinking how this must be what happens to the human spirit after death, after the struggle of life when male and female re-unite to become one again...in the Bible, in the beginning God is one being both male and female, but when God creates the two aspects of life they are divided to conform to the principles of creation...I am half dreaming and thinking about the universe and paradise in te wahi moemoeä, but it is te wahi kuku and then it is reality as Tania wakes up, lights up a cigarette and says she has to go away...because she won't be back there is nothing left for me in te wahi moemoeä...*"Thanks, Tony," says Hine and she walked up the path of her home without waiting for Paul.

"I don't envy you at all old boy!" Blunt says to him, "I'll give you a call if anything further comes up."

"Thanks Tony, and thank Cara. I'm sorry I spoiled such a lovely evening."

"Oh, that's all right, sometimes I wish Cara and I could get our feelings out like you working class chaps. If we have a tiff we just don't talk for days on end until at some point we're feeling so much we feel nothing at all. Then we just go out somewhere expensive and agree to call the whole thing off. Which is worse, fire or ice?"

"Don't touch me and don't talk to me!" Hine's eyes flashed at Paul as he walked into her room.

"Hine..." She covered her head with a pillow so she couldn't hear him. Calvert felt angry and he went over and pulled the pillow from her.

"I'll scream!" she said.

"Just listen to me for one minute and then I'll go!" They both realised the silliness of the situation and yet it was irreversible. Both of them had drawn their battle lines and had their defences up. Calvert felt he was the aggressor and the loser, all at once. Whatever he did or said could not make a difference, but he had to try.

"Hine..." he said softly as she sat silent and sullen, just going through the motions of listening to him so as to get rid of him, resenting his physical strength as well as his physical presence.

"Hine, I know what I did tonight was inexcusable, both hitting you and before that not telling you about all the things that happened to involve you in what is unfolding as a very sordid aspect of my past. I didn't tell you on the Sunday (it was only the day before yesterday but it seemed like a year ago now) because I couldn't get hold of you to begin with, and when I'd thought about it I didn't want to upset you unnecessarily by telling you over the phone. Then, when I did see you after work, well you know how we were -enjoying ourselves, and I just simply forgot - had I even thought about it I would have told you, but I was just happy to be with you. It's the first time I've been happy and relaxed for a long time - I just forgot."

Paul looked at Hine who she sat completely motionless with her eyes lowered, fixed on some object on the floor.

"And then," he continued, "I felt very upset by your attack on me about your being a Mäori, a woman, or both. I don't know who you've been talking to or where you those ideas, but I'm the last fucking person you should attack on those issues. Because that's all they are to some people, just bloody issues!!!"

He saw Hine looking at him out of the corner of her eye, but she quickly looked away again as she caught his eye.

"Some of these people with big ideas think no more of you than that you're just one of their 'issues' because you're a bloody Mäori or a woman or a one-legged dog or whatever, they string you along and you fall for it. But they won't be there you need real help as a human being, another lonely and washed out person who needs a bit of aroha just to stay alive. They'll all be off on another great cause by then, and you'll just be left . . ."

By this time Paul almost crying. He realised he was still haurangi and was getting irrational - all these things which he was accusing others of had also been levelled at himself in the past. He was so confused and exhausted that he felt all his physical strength draining away. But he went on ...

"And then the final thing which led to me hitting you was the fact that you were hitting me - I just wanted you to stop. Of course you weren't hurting me and I doubt whether I hurt you all that much, but it was just so annoying and I couldn't think of any way of making you stop. You would have gone on and on saying worse things about me, things which wouldn't have been true, and my friends would have been embarrassed and would have thought the worse of me. Of course the irony is now they must think I'm the lowest of the low - a woman-beater!"

Here he stopped and relented, he couldn't say any more. It was up to Hine now, he'd said all he could and as he watched her slowly raise her eyes towards him, Paul Calvert felt nothing but great shame and humiliation.

"I'm tired," she said. "Get out. I want to go to sleep and I don't want to see you again!"

When he finally heard these words from Hine he felt relieved, now he could get out of this terrible situation. Paul got up and walked out without saying a thing or turning to look at her. He crumpled up indifferently on the sofa and lay awake staring into the darkness. He felt like a concrete block and as he journeyed slowly towards a fitful, frequently interrupted sleep he could hear Hine crying wildly and heavily in the next room. Calvert too was crying inwardly, but his tears were like his heart, hard and dry and made of stone.

When Golly woke him in the morning with "Haere mai ki te mahi" Paul was almost glad to be going to work. For although he had a terrible hangover from the night before it would mean that he could take his mind off Hine and the evening's other events. When Golly threw a few jibes at him over sleeping on the couch Calvert just grunted, not feeling inclined to say anything about it. 'I'm sure he'll hear the story from Hine sooner or later,' he thought to himself. As the bus pulled into the Railway Station it started to pour down.

"Won't be doin' much today," said Hone.

They boarded the train and the journey to Mt. Eden seemed just a blurr, as had the bus trip from Ponsonby. Both men had to run about half a mile in what was, by this time, very heavy rain. They got to the depot where they found that only about half the gang had bothered to come to work. So Rua and Jimmy and Golly and Paul sat playing Manila and 'normal' poker, expecting any minute that the boss would be around to rain them off. When he finally did arrive about ten o'clock he said,

"Sorry boys, but we've got an urgent job, a burst water pipe over by Dominion Road. The Council boys have got their hands full so they gave me a call to see if we could do it. Of course, I thought we'd have a full gang, but if I give a hand I'm sure we'll get it done! It won't be for nothing either, you'll get a bit extra - Rua, give me the names of those who didn't turn up will you?"

When they got to the burst pipe it was really flooding the whole area, and a couple of properties were threatened. Paul got the job of digging around the break in order to clear any blockage that was in the pipe. It was really pissing down and Rua and Golly got to work to dig a channel in order to clear the excess water that was building up behind a stone retaining wall. About half an hour later they had the water running off down a local road and Calvert had all but cleared the blockage of clay and mud, and for the first time caught a glimpse of the broken pipe.

"It's in a bad way, eh!" said Rua "We got to replace about a metre of pipe - can't just cap that. Get that mixer going 'Culvert'!"

Calvert, who had by now been christened 'Culvert', which was slightly better than 'Pervert' and had the advantage of making his English surname sound more Irish, went up to the concrete mixer. It was dangerous using one of these in this weather even with a transformer, but it had to be done.

"Get the pipe cutters off the truck, 'Culvert', and then go with Jimmy and get a metre of pipe!"

They worked all that day and didn't finish until about six. The boss, Richard Moran, gave Paul a ride to Newmarket Station so he could get the last train to Manurewa.

"Well, that was a good day's work from you lot, I'll make it up to you. As for those who didn't come in, I think they'll be collecting their final pay tomorrow. Stupid bastards, all it means is they have to go back to Mt. Eden to finish their sentences instead of the freedom of the pre-release hostels. Nothing I can do about it though. If I start lying to the authorities about whether they came or not then I'm in the shit!"

"Richard," Paul said, - he now called the boss by his first name and also Rua and he had got on well after that day's hard work together (it's amazing how a common, shared difficult day's work can make men feel a certain comradeship in adverse conditions, where as before they had little or no respect for one another). "Richard, I'm staying with a friend and his sister at the moment and her husband is out of work, they're having a really hard time. They've got two kids and another one on the way and the dole doesn't really give them anything beyond survival. Also, he feels very bad about not working and there has already been one serious incident involving Rewi getting drunk and taking his frustration out on her. I'm sure he's a good worker, he's been made redundant on his last two jobs due to the freezing works closing down, and I'd like to be able to do something for them to repay their kindness for putting me up!"

As the boss's car turned into Broadway at the bottom of Khyber Pass, Richard Moran was silent, thinking over 'culvert's' proposition. It worried Paul that he was taking so long over his decision, but he didn't say any more, just let him think it through. Finally, as he stopped the car beside the pedestrian ramp that runs from Remuera down to Newmarket Station he said,

"Well Paul, thanks very much for your effort today. Bring your mate Rewi in to work in the morning. I'll be short tomorrow if I lay those off that didn't come in today. I don't like employing freezing workers all that much, they're usually lazy and nothing but trouble, just waiting around for the works to open again. However, this chap seems like he might be different, anyway I've got no choice - so long as he's not one of those bloody Union bastards - see you tomorrow."

"Thanks!" Paul said and watched the late model Jaguar disappear up Remuera Road towards his dream home in his dream suburb. As Paul walked down the ramp to the station he could see the light of the 6.30pm Auckland-Papakura train piercing through the mist and light rain. He felt extremely exhausted and was soaked to the skin. He realised most of the digging he had done that day had been in knee-high water and that the rest of the day had been spent out in pouring rain. Paul Calvert couldn't' wait to get home and have a hot bath and a good kai, and tell Rewi the news about his job.

For the next few weeks they settled into a rather routine life of going to work six days a week and just generally living a normal life, watching TV or reading in the evening. Rewi and Paul went to work every morning in the Mark II and usually came straight home, thus they both had a good effect on each other in terms of not drinking.

Elizabeth seemed happy and they all became close like a real whānau. Gradually with the effects of regular work and a healthier lifestyle Paul became quite fit, both physically and spiritually. None of the usual struggles of existence or problems of existential angst worried him during this time, and he even stopped dreaming to a large extent.

Of course this clearness of mind and sharpness of physical movement perturbed him somewhat at first. He felt almost like another person, but even though initially he tried to hang on to his degenerate past self, he couldn't fight the new regime and began to enjoy the benefits of fitness and health. Paul often thought of Hine and missed her and hoped she was alright. Hone was decidedly cool to him at work and they hardly said a word all day to each other. Hone always made sure he was working on a job that Calvert wasn't on and if they were on the same one Hone made sure he was mixing concrete while Paul was putting in the pipes or digging the trenches, or vice versa. Once Paul actually asked him how Hine was. "What you wanna know for, eh?" was all he said and then walked away.

Calvert also wondered from time to time about the people who had set him up on the dope deal. Who were they? Perhaps they were some neo-Nazi group like those that had been handing out pamphlets in the city recently advocating 'white rights etc.'

Perhaps it was someone playing a joke on him, someone who had known him in the Ponsonby drug days and heard he was back in town. Maybe it was the cops with nothing better to do on a Sunday afternoon. Anyway, whoever it was, it was now some time since he'd heard from them and the fact that he had destroyed the evidence meant that he couldn't even begin to take any action against them.

Calvert couldn't help, however, connecting them with the Mercedes which had been harassing him the first few days he had been in Auckland. Anyway, it had all been a few weeks ago now and the immediacy of all these events had faded into the realms of speculation and memory. Houston and Calvert were enjoying re-kindling their friendship. They would talk for hours on Sunday or sometimes after work, on books. Literature was his first love and it was good for him to be in the company of someone interested in ideas and feelings again. Eggars was a prolific writer by now and he would show Paul his poems and prose, and they would discuss them.

"You're really writing some good stuff, Eggars," Paul said as they sat in the living room one Saturday evening. Rewi and Elizabeth and the kids were all in bed. Rewi and Paul had worked up until about seven that evening fixing a sewer over by Mountain Road, and when they came home he was really tired. Elizabeth had tea ready for them and Rewi ate his, had a bath and went straight to bed. Liz was tired because of her pregnancy and she also went to early Mass on Sunday morning, which was a new departure for her from the Liz Eggars Calvert had known.

Instead of saying anything about Paul's comment on his writing Houston looked at his friend with a quizzical stare and after a minute or so he opened a large volume of what seemed to be someone's memoirs. Slowly he turned page after page until he came to what he was looking for.

"Here, read this. It's my father's diary which was published in Britain a couple of years ago." Paul took the book which was open at a chapter entitled 'Leading up to hostilities: Berlin before the war.' He took a sip of his cup of tea and began reading.

'On that night in 1938 I was invited by Calvert, who was enjoying something of a reputation as a scholar in Berlin, to join him and some other guests for dinner at Schader's hostel. Schader was a big Nazi party boss at the time and a minister in the Government, so I, as British Foreign Attaché, felt it my duty to attend. I had to go alone, as my wife was due to give birth in a week or so. However, I was accompanied by Joan Royce, the daughter of the Dean of Cambridge and a long-standing friend of our family. She had come to Berlin to try to persuade Calvert to marry her, as they had been lovers for some time, that being part of the reason for Calvert's coming to Berlin, to escape the ties she so desperately courted. She was staying with us and so we went together in a taxi. When we arrived at Schader's most of the party was already there . . .'

Here Paul interrupted his reading to say to Eggars,

"Your father's style is a bit turgid, and pedantic, is there any reason for me to go on reading this except that it's about my so called Uncle Roy?"

Eggars looked at his friend with a sly smile and said "Just read on MacDuff!"

Paul took another sip of tea and turned over a new leaf and read on, skipping over the more boring parts until he came to a part which amazed him.

'I was then introduced to a young Nazi chap by the name of von Klagen and also someone called Richard Calvert, whom I was told was Roy Calvert's brother. This I knew to be a lot of balderdash. However, I wisely kept that fact to myself. They were both with a beautiful young woman who seemed to have dark, almost Polynesian or Asian features, which was quite a novelty in the Berlin of the time. Her name was Mary O'Shea and she...'

Here Paul Calvert stopped reading, being totally dumbfounded by this mention of his mother's name. Eggars was watching him, knowing what a shock it would be to find out that Paul's mother had been involved with both his fathers at this early stage, and that she had been in Berlin with them. Calvert was about to berate Eggars for not warning him when he said,

"Go on reading Paul, there's more!" So he read on with such a mixture of feelings he could hardly read properly, but these settled after a while as he read,

'Mary O'Shea was a beautiful young woman who seemed extraordinarily close to the two men, Calvert's brother and von Klagen. Apparently, it was a relationship that was notorious throughout Berlin, even drawing the attention of Himmler himself. Of course, I was again not to be closely associated with these people, but Herr Schader certainly seemed charmed by the threesome. There was one particular incident during that evening at the Adlon Hotel which stuck in my mind and since the war I have found out an explanation for this curious event. I had been down one end of the dinner table discussing various political issues which had arisen since the Nazis had assumed power.

'Lewis Eliot, a Cambridge Fellow working for the British Government; was arguing against the new regime somewhat too vehemently in the circumstances I felt. Joan had taken Roy home early and there were only the six of us left. Suddenly, the intensity of the political row was superseded by a personal one involving the terrible trio, all of whom were exceedingly drunk at the time. Von Klagen was holding a photograph of himself and saying to Calvert, "There is no need to be jealous, Richard, I am giving Mary a photograph of myself not for personal reasons but because it contains a code." "Sure ta Christ you're a layer!" said Calvert, whose real name I have since found out was O'Hanlon - both he and Mary O'Shea were working for the I.R.A., procuring arms from the Germans. "Give ta me ta photo or ile smash ya in ta gob!" said Calvert and he took a wild swing at von Klagen, who pulled away and Calvert went sprawling on the floor.

'Apparently this was a regular feature of their nights out together in Berlin. Anyway, Schader excused himself from our conversation and went over to von Klagen, and after a brief argument von Klagen and Miss O'Shea picked up Calvert-O'Hanlon and left. Schader returned to the table saying "You must excuse my young colleagues behaviour gentlemen. Von Klagen is a very talented young officer in the Reich. Unfortunately, due to the nature of his work he has to mix with an unsavoury element of humanity. It's bad enough that Calvert's half-brother is Irish, but that woman has some kind of negro blood from the other side of the world - quite distasteful - now, where were we? Oh yes! The purification of the world by the Aryan race!" Leaving the party not long after...'

At this point Paul put down the book. He couldn't help himself and burst out laughing. Eggars must have thought he'd gone crazy for he just laughed and laughed and laughed, the tears streaming down his cheeks. He was laughing and crying, and then away laughing again about the fact that he was laughing and crying. Calvert was thinking of father O'Hanlon saying to my mother. "You're just like the Maoris. You don't know whether you're laughing or crying," and here he was laughing and crying a generation later, because of those two, the people who looked after him and loved him and cared for him all those years. The fact that she was Māori just seemed to make it even funnier. And he was thinking how he didn't even know them.

There they were in Berlin in 1938 spying and getting drunk and jealous, and father O'Hanlon taking a swipe at father von Klagen because he was giving the woman they both loved a photograph which had some sort of coded message and which Paul Calvert found on his dead mother's body as he went to wake her up one morning with a nice cup of tea in Orakei, a suburb in Auckland. It was all too much and there he was laughing and crying "just like the Maoris" on a Saturday evening in Manurewa, and what was going to happen next?

Dreamland was remote and aloof. He couldn't go back there now. He couldn't even dream about going there! He thought of Hine but she too was far away. He couldn't reach her because she didn't want him to. He tried to think about how she was feeling, was she all right, was she upset or happy? But his mind moved back to the absurdities of his parents, the total up-turning of his past.

"Well, what do you think of that Calvert?" said Eggars after his friend had been

silent for a good five or ten minutes.

"I don't know what to think, Houston. I just don't know any more. It seems that as the days go by while I'm here in Auckland more and more weird things turn up about my past until I just don't know where I stop and the world begins."

"Let's go for a ride," said Eggars. "Maybe that'll clear your thoughts a bit and we can have a talk about things after that. I'll get the keys!"

He went out to the kitchen and Calvert went to his room and put on a jacket. It was a cold night but the rain had stopped and as the Mark II pulled out of the driveway they could see stars twinkling in the sky. By the time they reached the motorway on-ramp, feeling the wind caused by the rush of the car, Paul was beginning to feel better, more physical and alive. The Zephyr belted along the motorway, enjoying the head-on confrontation with the west wind.

They nearly spun-out at Tip Top Corner, a time honoured custom with Aucklanders, and as they approached the Newmarket Viaduct their car was almost flying.

A car going south flashed its headlights on and off, another Auckland tradition to warn on-coming drivers that there's a cop up ahead. So as they entered the spaghetti twists and turns that the motorway takes through Grafton Gully they slowed down to the speed limit just in time to see a cop car sitting on the side of the Symonds Street off-ramp.

"Saturday night, everything's alright here on Radio Hauraki, Auckland's number one! Now we go back in time with the Drifters, 'Saturday Night at the movies', who cares what picture you see, Yeah!"...*this is Auckland's Pirate Radio, Radio Hauraki broadcasting from the Tiri in the Hauraki Gulf...we hope you heard our first ever song 'Born Free', a very apt tune for New Zealand's first Private Radio Station...just like our sister stations in the U.K. such as Caroline we are here break the monopoly of the public air-waves...so here is the second song of the new era in broadcasting for our country...The Beatles, 'Yellow Submarine' - but it'll take more than the lowering of a drawbridge to make us into a submarine - "In the town where I was born"*...the Mark II rattled on through the town where Paul Calvert was born and they turned off the motorway at Nelson Street and then down Cook Street into Queen Street.

The main street was a madhouse. Cars and bikes jostled for room all up and down the length of this lit-up thoroughfare through the city. Slowing down, and with their elbows out the window and the radio blaring, Eggars and Paul cruised the main street in mock-cool heroic style. The footpaths were overflowing with people of all shapes and sizes because the movies had just finished. They turned right into Customs Street, and went along past the bus depot and then right into Fort Street by the bottom of Emily Place.

As they slowly rode along Fort Street Paul realised that this area was now a little sister to Karangahape Road who had set up shop after dark in competition with the older sister, because the family had become too big to support her now. So Fort Street fleshed and flashed out its neon slogans 'Nude this,' 'Nude that' and 'Nude a bit of the other!' Eggars stepped on the gas and they almost rolled into Queen Street. He straightened up the car and drove very fast through a red light at the bottom of Wyndham Street.

Calvert remembered how he'd done a similar stunt round the Octagon in Dunedin on a visit from Parimoana one time. 'Hooning round the Octagon' was the local term, or at least that's what the cop that pulled him up had called it. With this in mind Paul pointed out a cop sitting on his bike up the road a bit, as they waited at the lights at the Victoria Street intersection.

"We'll fix him!" said Eggars, and he pulled the car out of the middle lane into the right-turn lane. This put them a car length ahead of any other cars and right in the middle of the pedestrian crossing. Their tyres screeched as they turned into Victoria Street West, and they could just see the cop' s head turn towards them before they were out of sight. They got some gas at the Downtown Service Station and then headed for the Harbour Bridge.

Zooming down the Shore side of the bridge and past where the toll gates used to be Eggars said "Well, Paul, I was talking to Liz today and she said that she and Rewi are getting on really well now that he's got a job – she's very grateful to you."

"I'm the one that's grateful - if I hadn't found a stable place to live I'd be a real mess by now! All I've got to do now is try and piece all this bloody stuff about my family together. I've lost touch with my brother and sisters, I don't know where they are. Now I've got all this weird information about my background and I don't know what to do. I'm being chased or followed by some bastards in a black Mercedes. I get dope planted on me and then nearly get busted for it. Hine tells me to fuck off - I don't know what's going on in this crazy city."

They continued driving to the end of the motorway, then cut across through Albany over towards Greenhithe where the Upper Harbour Bridge brought them through Hobsonville and then on to the North-Western Motorway back towards the city. By this time Paul Calvert was feeling a bit tired, but enjoying just driving through the night with the radio going, talking away to Eggars.

A song comes on the radio - an old reggae-calypso type song which has the last few lines 'My mama - said go man go! Your daddy ain't your daddy but your daddy don't know! Woe is me, shame and scandal in de family.'

"Pretty appropriate song for you, Paul." Calvert just smile at Eggars' remark. They were passing through the Pt Chev turnaround and Paul couldn't help thinking how this motorway has carved up areas which would seem to be tapu. Here it passes through what used to be a large area of Carrington Hospital's front yard.

"That place must be a madhouse with the motorway going through it like that." Eggars grins and yells "Three!" as they pass through Chamberlain Park Golf Course.

"Funny how they got rid of almost all the Catholic graveyard when they put the Southern Motorway through Grafton Cemetery. Must be Freemasons in the Planning Department !" Calvert mused. They went for a quick burn down to the end of the Southern Motorway and then turned around made their way home to Manurewa.

When they got in the door there was a message for Paul to ring Inspector BrianWilkinson of the Otahuhu Police immediately. He was really puzzled and felt anxious and slightly nauseated.

"What do they want?" He wondered aloud.

"Only one way to find out," said Eggars. It turned out that Wilkinson was the older police officer who had been around that Sunday a few weeks ago to bust Calvert for the dope. Paul had completely forgotten his name.

"Well Calvert," the cop said, "that's as much as I want to say on the phone. I'll send Johnson and a colleague around to get you straight away. I must say I was disappointed you didn't phone me up like I asked you to. Anyway, I hope what I've said is of interest and that we can go into things a bit more thoroughly when I see you."

"Well?" said Eggars, as he handed Paul a cup of coffee. Calvert told him what Wilkinson had said. Apparently there were many more police records on his father O'Hanlon than just the one for petty theft. When he died there was a warrant out for his arrest on treason charges related to his work for the I.R.A. during the war. Similar charges had been laid in train against Paul's mother. If Paul hadn't read Eggars senior's diary earlier that evening he would not have understood that at all. Not only that. Wilkinson had discovered an article in a West German magazine which alleged that von Klagen, a former SS Colonel, had escaped to the antipodes with a vast fortune and many secret documents which could be used to incriminate dozens of leading German businessmen in relation to their Nazi past.

"His escape" Wilkinson had continued reading from the paper, "had been made possible by two close friends whose names are unknown, but who had been working with von Klagen throughout the war for the Irish Nationalists. Von Klagen had also left Germany with top secret coded messages designed to help the escape of SS men and women should Hitler's war not succeed."

These things were going around in Paul's mind when Johnson and a plain clothes 'D' came to the door. Paul got in the car and as they drove off he was about to ask Johnson about the other things that Wilkinson alluded to on the phone. At this point the 'D' pulled out a gun and knocked him unconscious with the butt! When he came to Calvert had a headache equal to any of his biggest hangovers. He tried to move but his hands were tied to an old piece of machinery which overhung a shallow pit. The room was in was a large warehouse or disused woolstore. It was very dark, except over in one corner where a light came from an office from which came hushed talk. Two or three

people were having a discussion which would have been an argument if they had not been so careful in trying to keep their voices down.

"Prepare the needle!" Calvert heard a guttural, harsh sound from someone obviously used to giving orders. Then one of the people in the room came over the concrete floor towards Paul Calvert.

"I trust you had a pleasant sleep, mein jungen von Klagen?" As the man went to untie his hands Calvert realised that he had referred to him in his biological father's name. The man spoke in a German accent and he took Calvert at gunpoint across the factory floor towards the light of the office. Paul realised that it was the young 'detective' who had hit him on the head when he and Johnson had come to take him to the Police Station. Paul Calvert was confused and genuinely puzzled and not just because of the blow and waking up in this strange place.

The fact that this 'D' talked in a German accent and that he called him von Klagen really had his mind at a blank. The 'D' pushed him into the office and there was Johnson, no longer in a Police uniform but in a uniform which approximated that of an SS Colonel, the type worn by a European neo-Nazi group that Calvert had read about in a magazine. Paul's first reaction was to laugh as he saw Johnson preparing a needle of heroin, holding it upright and giving it that final squirt before administering it to what Paul thought would be his own arm. There was third man who sat at a table. He was older, about sixty or seventy and he was obviously the authority.

"Guten Abend, Herr von Klagen," he said. "I haf waited eins long time for this occasion. Do sit down."

The young 'D' pushed Paul into a chair and retreated to stand guard at the door.

"I see you find something amusing about our gathering. Perhaps you can let us in on your little joke, ja!"

Calvert didn't have any strength or inclination to try to explain his reason for laughing, so sat there silently, not knowing what was going to happen next, only wishing he could be back in the safety of dreamland. After a short while the older man who had been sitting facing him stood up and walked slowly around the table. Paul noticed that he too had a uniform on, only this time it was the real thing. Here he was in a bloody old wool-store or whatever somewhere in Auckland in the nineteen eighties and he was about to he interrogated by a bloody SS Officer of the Third Reich - it was fucking ridiculous, he just wanted to laugh or cry or wake up - or something, anything. But all he could do was sit in stunned silence while he heard this voice saying -

"Vell!-Nefer mind, I could nefer understant humour anyvay! Now, mein freund, ve must talk you and I. I belief you haben sie, you vill excuse my English ist still bad. You are Paul von Klagen, son of a certain von Klagen who vas my colleague in sa SS and who now lives somewhere in this city. I haf for many years now been trying to find your farter, und not just for old times sake!"

Here he paused. His tone was changing. Instead of patronising he was becoming angry. Paul was glad the Nazi had stopped because he was trying to assimilate this latest revelation that his father lived in Auckland, and it was difficult to think and listen to this bastard booming away in his ear at the same time. The Nazi continued, only in a more relaxed style of speaking,

"Now, Herr von Klagen, your farter has somethink that I very much vont. It is just eine small thing only it means a lot to me. It is just a photograph of someone that I know - in fact it is a photograph of himself - your farter. Vell, I'll tell you, it ist not for sentimental reasons I have risked my life to come here, twelf thousand miles. I haf been eine vanted man since 1945. Nein! I haf comen here becaus that photograph contains a coded message from Martin Borman about de vere ist hidden plans to restore the glorious Reich of our Fatherland, which is now difvided and corrupted on vun side by shabby bolshevism, and on the other side by decadence und capitalist corruption. Along wif these plans ist also a fortune of gold bullion vich vill be used to karry out these wishes of our Fuhrer." After a short pause he continued.

"Somehow your incompetent fool of a farter mixed that photograph code up vif eine similar one he had when he was dealing also vif those murderers from the Irish Republik!"

Calvert could no longer contain his laughter, not just the idea of a Nazi calling the I.R.A. murderers, but because he had this image of his two fathers, drunk as devils, fighting over the woman they loved whilst on top secret assignments for their respective organisations and masters. His German father gives the wrong message to his mother, who is also drunk and also a spy, and she thinks it's a gift for her and keeps it hidden from his Irish father so as not to hurt him. When she died he finds her clutching it to her breast, and now it is with his things out in Manurewa. A baton thumped across Paul's face. As the pain increased he heard whoever this Nazi is call,

"Bring that here, now! Schnell!" Johnson brought over the injection he had prepared. "Perhaps you vont be lafing soon, my young freund."

He then roughly jabs the needle into Paul's arm.

Calvert felt the pleasure pain run through his veins. He had never taken smack and never wanted to, but now here it was running through the rivers and canals, surging along. He remembered all his friends who had overdosed and felt terrified, but the stuff was also making him feel real good and he was floating although he was in chains. He was a free captive, and when the Nazi bastard said . . .

"Tie him up – let's get out of here, Schnell! Schnell!" Calvert himself was laughing and flying as they tied him back on to what he had been previously tied to, only now they had him in the pit. They had tied his hands to a piece of machinery overhead so that he couldn't sit down. Calvert was like a hanging carcass and he loved it.

"We vill be back tonite, ja! I think you vill like to haben sie eine talke by zen!"

As a parting gesture he whacked Paul Calvert in the back with his baton. Paul's body reacted but he didn't feel a thing. When the three Nazis left Paul was calm for a while, just enjoying hanging from his wrists in the dark, his feet barely touching the ground. He began thinking about how he could get some more smack. It was so good he wondered why he ever thought of it so negatively before. So what if you died, nothing in life could be better than this anyway. It must be the ultimate way to go.

Then a division forced itself in his mind. Why was he thinking like this? It was ludicrous, hanging from some fucking machine in the middle of an empty factory and being questioned by Nazis who wanted to get hold of a photograph he'd found on his dead mother and all he could do is laugh and enjoy being out of it on some drug he had always despised. What about Tania, the way he'd seen her right out of it crying and pleading, what about Debbie, Billy and all the others who had died? And here he was saying how it didn't matter. It didn't matter if he died and it didn't matter that they'd died...*ko kau te maramatanga i tenei ao pouri...*"What's that, who said that?" *Calvert called out in fright...she had plenty beer by the time her man humiliated her...I didn't know what was going on...has reached you from eternity...he was struggling to make sense but his mind was off - the drug was taking me for a little trip...and as with the stone...I began to disconnect...I look at...I try to focus on something external, the place is getting lighter, it must be getting towards daytime but I am entering the night - I picked up my gun...all the windows were blacked over so that everything remained dark even though you could tell it was day, te po, te po, te po nui, Hine nui te po sits waiting for everyone, through her you leave the world, the same way you enter...e tahi ra koe mau e mohio au, a puaki te taha au...*"Ring Warren Walker - you ring it"*...after a time we left Okahu Bay...this evening you were the moon to me...dark night, wind off the harbour...on a train journey back from dreamland, now back to dreamland in a vein...I find out that the woman and man were put...were put, what doesn't make sense, were put! I realise I am arguing with my own thoughts - am I going mad? All these things moving through my mind so disjointed...it's not your...I just don't know, the night-mare world of the heroin is swamping me, it's not altogether unpleasant, but I just don't know my own thoughts, I feel physically good even though I'm in pain from hanging...but my mind is off the rails, or maybe on a completely different set of dreaming/flying rails, I don't know...me nga awa o te tonga...I think how curious it is that when I get drunk my conversation becomes interspersed by Māori and now I'm on this* *drug my thoughts are also in Mäori as much as English...another person gone porangi against the urgent call...am I thinking about myself with that thought?...mataku ki kia au aroha koe, i mataku e taka au...I am lost, I abandon myself to the sleep of reason, the faithful birds of thought and creatures of the night world will take their pleasures in the fields and sky of my mind, te wahi moemoeä, te wahi kuku...in dreams I walked...half beautiful, half fearsome...taua ki haere rä, a po muringa te haerenga i runga i te tereina...you exist for me as He does for you...kore raro hui atu mokemoke, me kia au puritia...some reference to her being number two woman...darkness of self - of unremembered soul...I mean, this war has killed love...you don't know anything...is like each wave of water...your beauty is so strong that I weep inward...3, stab No; 4 Stab; 8 Stab; 3 Stab;...of remembering an Auckland phone number...we would all go to the movies and then meet mum...at the point of sundown and the rising darkness I see you...te Marama hangere, kua ahau ngaro i te kapua...ka te pouri au, kua wareware te ngakau...stand between us like trees against the horizon...an hour before I had seen her in the dining car...I was a stranger in a familiar land...one day you may know who I am...(they all remind me of you) against the station door as a means...was the small flicker of flame mentioned a fur coat-wrapped woman...from falling on the floor, from being kicked out of bed...and once again my dreams shatter pera ki ia, ngaru o te wai...where people, scurrying like rats ka tuturi...this karanga is pulling at my heart exposing the sadness below the surface...e rite au ki te tangata e ki ana I let you walk ahead so you would not see me...retreat to the never-changing beauty of dreamland...rang out across the platform when he, with another woman in mind (and my lovers I also see) but without a map to the south...I just saw a couple of cops talking to my brother...e hara nau te he ko te one o taku tamarikitanga, te one oranga (found it the other day) my lovers, were they really here (long ago is far away)...can I have an articulated truck for Christmas...the moon, cut in half, hidden by clouds when I saw you in the hall of mirrors (how can my mother be a memory) ran in all directions towards survival together they make a flood of tears anyone could belong to the coffee club it was my single purpose but I could not hold you as a woman...which I look at kei ahau he poke i roto i taku manawa a wairua and you will come to me...*the thoughts became less distinct as the pain increased. The pain of Calvert's wrists was just about unbearable. He had all his weight hanging from them and the skin was now raw and blood was dripping on to his head and nose and forehead. But even more than this was the pain of the need for more heroin - the desperate longing, also he was beginning to experience mild withdrawal symptoms for although he had only one shot it must have been quite a large dose and his body now needed more to keep it going on the same level.

He tried to call out but his voice was so faint and dry that he gives up and soon falls unconscious with pain and despair. When he comes to this time he is sitting in a chair back in the office room.

CHAPTER 4

The first thing Paul Calvert sees when he regains consciousness is Johnson fixing up another injection and he just about goes off his head. A sense of optimism takes over his whole being and he knows that as soon as he has a fix everything will be all right. He makes grabbing motions towards the needle but soon realises he is strapped into the chair.

"Now von Klagen, are you ready to talk, ja!"

Paul asks if he can go to the toilet first and then things will be more pleasant for everyone. Calvert's first ever armed escort to a toilet takes place and he can't help but laugh when Kruger, the 'D', says,

"No funny business" and Calvert gets a whack in the mouth for his pains. Upon his return he notices that the symbol of the three wise monkeys is emblazoned on the Nazi boss's bag, minus the swastikas.

"So, you're the three monkeys," Calvert says with an ironic tone that only people with a sense of humour could apprehend.

"I suppose you were the ones following me around in a Mercedes, taking pictures and all that?"

The boss's ears pricked up. "Nein!" He turned to Kruger and asked him something in German "Nein!" replied Kruger.

"Herr Johnson did you know of this?"

"No, I didn't Herr..."

"Shut up you fool, you don't want this Klagen to know who I am." Leaving the others, the Nazi boss came close to me and said,

"Perhaps our guest is hafing another of his humour wif us." He hit Paul with his baton and said,

"That is not so funny is it! Now, vere ist the foto und who ist in the Mercedes?"

Paul Calvert was in great pain and completely exhausted - he was screaming in a hoarse voice that he wanted his shot.

"You vill haben sie alles der shot you vant ven you tell us vere ist der fotograf." But Paul remained silent. He didn't want them breaking in on Liz and Rewi and he didn't even want them to have the photograph - it was bad enough people like this were alive let alone alive with enough money and power to run other people's lives. But his resolve was weakening as he saw Johnson hold the needle upright and squirt a small amount out in preparation for injecting him. Calvert was craving the drug by this time and must have been acting like he was, for the boss came over to him and grabbed his hair, pulling it up so all Paul could see was his large, cruel face. The Nazi smiled and said

"I believe you have a fraulein, ja! Some black bitch - well, I shouldn't be surprised to hear that it doesn't mean much vot happens to her, am I right? A man of gut German stock like yourself wouldn't really care vot happens to a black girl - ja!?"

"My mother was black!" Calvert cried with force. "You keep your hands off Hine, you filthy bastard."

"Ve vill see! Johnson!" Johnson came over and put the needle in Calvert's arm. All the pain left and everything became quite beautiful. Even the Nazi's parting kick in the head felt good.

"I vant this cleared up by tomorrow - I haf to leave New Zealand on Tuesday und tonight ist Sunday already!"

The Nazi boss turned threateningly to Calvert, saying

"You better haf an answer tomorrow or I won't be able to stop the vorst happening to you und your girl - black girl!"

They left Paul as they had the previous night. His wrists were like raw meat now, but he had his heroin and he was all right. For a while he hung there blissfully not thinking, just feeling good to be hanging. But this time the distorted state of mind came on a lot quicker and because he knew what was going on this time he didn't fight it by wondering what it was. However, this time was far more nightmarish because he couldn't get Hine off his mind. It was darker and a lot colder on this night and the pain shot from his wrist in waves through his whole body. "Hine!" he called out. He was responsible for anything that happened to her because of this...kua pouri, ka pupuki te hau this ol' photograph...far worse than anything Rommel dished up...despite the amount we'd had to drink I didn't know where I was, Hine held me close...Calvert tried to hold his thoughts, to focus on one thing - but the night without was as dark as the night within, and he couldn't see anything, either with his mind's eye or with his natural eye. He could only experience pain and terrifying thoughts of madness as his mind floated freely on the sea of heroin...I didn't know the timetable...through crowded confused streets...I jumped aboard...an old photograph...(Or were they always you)...the photograph was of three men in their mid –twenties...pera i te marama kahuna kou i...another person gone porangi I thought...kaere au i mohio ana...otira rete he tamaiti tangohia ia tahi hikoi...precious and hidden...while studying at Trinity he was actually using his position...as she used deliberate, violent stabs with her fingers...the only pure light in a life of shadows...fault that I...of midnight at Taihape station...the war which can never be won...I was a bit taken aback but I wanted to be sure...I must have been drunk to want to sleep with you...scotta ice now wanna beer...as the child is afraid of falling...listening to a poet reading poetry who in my life is like...I am afraid of saying I love you...my beautiful flaxen-haired lover what happened...I didn't know you could speak Japanese brother...a i taku rapu haere ia koe, ko ngaro au...this karanga of the Polynesian woman through a human fog...kept me from going insane...didn't know...we were about to step out off the footpath...we made love gently and after Hine had gone to sleep I lay awake for a while...it was as though he was watching his own thoughts going by like on one of those electronic screens down by the South Pacific Hotel which tells you the news and about Canons etc. As he watched these thoughts building in their intensity Paul realised they were more and more about Hine. He was now in a completely devastated, exhausted and hedonistic state and yet his mind, through its random thought processes was sorting out priorities. As he gave way to total abandonment of his debauched moral self he could also see the natural attrition of reality forcing its way through his amoral state...go away, you all the same...in my uniform I watched the beauty of ko te maramatanga hei oranga, kahore mo te aroha she had called out laughing; getting ready to cry...remorseless, unseen gaze of the Māori Chief statue...I have a hole in my heart and spirit kei te mokemoke au under mountains...you really got my sis mad...he rite ki te pounamu kahurangi kei hia koe i ngaro nei hoping you and your child would embrace me...not today my presumed father answered the sky turned turquoise from blue over the white, white landscape the moon too hid behind a veil e ngare hore kau he tohutohu then kiss the ground pretty hoha, she kissed me, she sat silently not an expression on her face hurihuri ngä pohutukawa ko te po te awhi i taku kitenga we said goodnight after the journey on the train te moemoeä te kuku this Tamaki Makaurau you carry the weight of my passion, what do you want for a kai imbecile and went outside where things weren't quite drowning the cries of the heart where to look what we gonna do asked Hine, come and sleep with me tonight e Paul in the dark I am alone with the old memories "This is quite good on TV" you only arrived back in Auckland a few days ago Bob Marley and I make Hine's canoe like all the other victims hui katoa, ka heke o te manawa on a sinking ship she smiled at me and left the room she is my only solace the darkness like a miner provides the only natural light your husband and your children a single sound moving through the pathways of the past then he ordered his men to shoot sis will be angry if you're late I think of you, I think of you I became lost, Hine laughed and then got us a drink I never been anywhere in Remuera before with a passion te marama ki ahau and isolated rivers minutes to spare sachet of white powder 6 stab 2 stab 4 stab and we head towards in dreams I moved you radiated decay an ahei te pupuri koe tawhite he wahine when Hine saw this she cracked up laughing looks like you she said like the rhythmic call of an ancient chant kei tenei anake te maramatanga ke ata papakihia mai e ngä ngaru a wae ano taku mamoe maungamonga i raro i te mana kaupapa our love cannot be of this world she'd gone pale drenching downpours trying not to make a sound or a movement nestled amongst several dozen edifices and she ran to you as if I were a stranger a tank drove by to my thoughts blandly saying now I'm talking to junior in the Dining Car, I am alone soon the whole area will be covered what you take me for a stupid Māori then I said how's things Liz in my search for you through the hard-nosed life of a labouring man the ground of my childhood, the ground of my life ko wai kei i roto i taku ora the greenstone sun rising over the horizon of the sea I whacked Hine like your master's kingdom so grim to find the child whom I love all my lovers are memories now ring Warren Walker - ring it made me vulnerable Elizabeth's tirade now get out I never want to see you again I'd like to tell you now that you are definitely under suspicion...suddenly the rapid staccato thought-upon-thought pace of his mind stopped.

Everything was dark and Calvert's physical agony, though intense, seemed distant. He felt as if he was drowning in a dry sea, a sea of air and in that air he could see the crossings, unlevel and indistinct, between his past, future and present; drowning on the surface, but every so often going down for air 'a la giacon', as they say...that kept me and...I felt that I was almost dead, the last vestiges of life were draining from my being...idly to myself...no longer the flowing torrent of dis-unified thoughts but rather...Hinengaro Te Riro i He I have carried you with me all day...the slow meandering of a wide and deep river-life moving...a ama ki te pounamu, the koha of Taihape between trains, the first time ever I (get me to the doctor, the dolphins! The Dolphins!) and all our other heroes we can be, if God will protect us, you and me ...moving towards an eternal sea of death...ka mahue ngä pohutukawa...I was completely indifferent to my fate, I felt nothing for life, I felt nothing for death, (death, schmeath) I was only drifting...i ngaro nei i waho i ngä maunga...I thought of Rangi, I thought of Tania and Melissa, I thought of Hine with her full name, all my jumbled thoughts of the heroin dreams had centred on them...but you turned away...and Miranda and my mother and Aroha, I thought it strange that all the women, all the female elements had come to visit me and haunt me...which lit this poem in my heart...I heard a strange sound that sounded like hoot-hoot...this ol' memory...then I heard it again, I knew it was the call of the morepork, the Mäori sign that death was about to occur...te Ruru-whekau, nö reira; a real hoot and I was a child taking my first step...now I knew why the women's spirits had gathered around me, they were there to remind me of who brought me into this world and also how I would leave - they had brought me the message of Hine-nui-te-po, I would enter the spirit world the same way I had entered this world, through a woman...the sadness of each memory...the morepork called again and I knew it was real...as you approach the sand...I was struck with terror! I wanted to live! I wanted to see, and feel and touch and love, I wanted to move...your image leapt at me, is now here to stay...lying in the darkened bedroom as the first light of dawn began to rise slowly above the darkness, Hinengaro Te Riro i He, if you want another kind of love I'll wear a mask for you who realised the enormity...and the necessity of what had happened...drifting between dreams and sleep and future betrayal, she found herself wandering alone along a desolate beach...now I felt the coming down again from the smackdream, the withdrawal and the need, the degradation and pain of the need, I couldn't do anything - maybe I had died and gone to hell but another call from the morepork told me I was still alive and he had become her. The ruru was calling louder and more often, as if it were on some kind of rostered schedule, mai i te moana, even if she didn't survive herself, that baby must! With all her remaining strength Hinengaro jerked her legs painfully from under the wooden beam which held her. And with a great effort of will she freed herself...each wave that laps at your feet...the colours, the heat and the pain all intensified as she staggered towards the direction she had come from...having just enough energy to call out, 'te aroha ki tena, ki tena' another flash but it wasn't that easy...she coughed violently, yelling, "HELP!" and as the foggy smoke billowing image embraced her, she collapsed and everything went black...he held his arms outstretched, ka wehe mal i Okahu kei te awake au deep and dark i tenei ahiahi ko koe, Paul Calvert couldn't call out, he couldn't see, his thoughts began to jump and jumble again and the morepork called woowoo ruuruu, then a loud bang and a great flash of light and everything went blank.

CHAPTER 5

The first face Paul Calvert saw when he regained consciousness was Inspector Wilkinson's. The cop was standing talking to a nurse and doctor and as soon as Calvert made a sound approximating human language the Inspector broke off his conversation and came over to his bed.

"Feeling better, Calvert? We thought we'd lost you for a while there."

Hine and Golly were on the other side of the bed and Hine kissed him gently on the forehead. Both his arms were bandaged and were held in place by clamps so he couldn't move them. Paul tried to sit up but the doctor said, "I'm afraid you must stay as you are for a few days – you're still in quite bad way."

Wilkinson then sat next to him and told him what had been going on. Paul kept looking at Hine throughout the policeman's talk and she was also looking at him, pleased to see him he thought. On the Saturday when Johnson didn't come back to Otahuhu with Calvert, Wilkinson, who had apparently had some suspicions about Johnson, made a general police alert throughout the Auckland area that evening. Calvert then remembered certain things that Wilkinson had said during the Manurewa raid and the way Johnson had been so eager to get him off with Wilkinson. However, there had been a lot of trouble at Aotea Square that night and the police had been over-stretched, so not much could be done that evening. Paul was about to ask Golly if Skids had been involved but thought the better of it because there was a cop there.

"On Sunday," Wilkinson continued, "we stepped up our esquires to a full-scale manhunt. I'm afraid at that point I was thinking that you and Johnson might have been working in collusion - you were still under suspicion as a drug dealer and I thought maybe you had joined with Johnson, and that would have been a real head-ache. You see we had known of Johnson's corruption as a police officer for some time, but we didn't want to move on him since we thought he might lead us to the big fish."

At this point the nurse came over to Wilkinson and explained that Calvert was still very weak. Wilkinson said, "Yes, of course, but if Calvert doesn't mind, I've still got one or two questions. I'll return tomorrow for a fuller interview."

Paul intimated that he felt alright and so Wilkinson asked him if he had actually been involved with drug dealing. When he answered no, the cop said,

"As I thought! Now, during the last couple of days you've been in hospital you've been quite delirious a lot of the time."

"Yeah, you saying some pretty porangi things, Paul. It was funny listening to you, eh."

Hine was beautiful to him just then. He wanted to take her in his arms and love her, but he was happy enough to listen to her voice, the beauty of her spirit. He'd been talking a lot about the neo-Nazis who had held him captive. He'd spoken a lot of unintelligible Mäori, but most of all he'd talked about the morepork and his imminent death.

"Where we found you, in one of those old abandoned woolsheds in the Strand at the back of the Railway Station, is a highly unlikely place for a morepork. Even if there was one, it would very difficult to hear it on a Monday morning. Now Calvert, where were we?" said Wilkinson...George and I were late for work as usual, we were working in this wool store down at the bottom of Parnell Rise and we walked from College Hill every morning...we were pressing bales to make double bales for export to Russia...we would wheel the bales into the press and there was a student wheeling off...the machinery was old and every now and then the press would fly open before the wire had been fixed around it and two five hundred pound bales would come flying out at us...one time this happened and the student, who still had his wool-hook in his hand, nearly gouged his eye out when he put his hand up to protect himself...they took him off to hospital and I went to the boss to demand the press be shut down, and he threatened to sack me...I told him I'd go straight to the Department of Labour and have him shut down for operating unsafe machinery...I watched this unscrupulous little weasel of a man pick up his phone and tell his engineer to close down the press...as I stood there in a cloud of his cigar smoke, I heard the hoot-hoot of a train leaving Auckland Station...Wilkinson had been giving more details about how he had come to the conclusion that these Nazis had been dealing in drugs world-wide to finance their return to power. His theories had been confirmed by recent contacts he'd had with Interpol.

Suddenly Paul Calvert burst out laughing.

"Morepork! Morepork!" he shouted. Everyone looked astonished and thought he'd gone porangi.

"If you found me in that bloody deserted warehouse - well I used to work there years ago before I went to dreamland, and all day I remember the trains would be leaving, blowing their whistles twice, hoot-hoot, that must be my bloody morepork!"

Everyone laughed at such an absurd profundity and then the nurse came in saying they all had to leave because the patient was still weak and too much excitement would be bad for him.

Paul Calvert was able to leave hospital within a week and a half. While he had been there Hine had come to see him every night after work. She seemed very pleased that things had brought them together again. The two of them talked for hours about how they should get back together, how much they enjoyed being with each other. A couple of days before Paul was due to leave Auckland Hospital, Hine was visiting him. It was a beautiful night and from his bed he could see right across the harbour, all the city lights and the steady flow of traffic over the bridge.

"Better come and stay with me Paul, eh. Liz has got enough on without a sick adult too!"

He wasn't expecting this. He was half delighted and half apprehensive.

"Are you sure you feel okay about that, Hine?" he said. She assured him that she did and added,

"We in this together now Paul!" He realised that she wasn't just being nice or taking him off Liz's hands, but that she really did want them to be together and share everything that came their way. He was about to give lot of arguments against her being so committed to them. He'd still be danger from those Nazis, he had to find out about his father who was still alive and living in New Zealand, he had to be off work for a while yet, he wouldn't be able to use his arms for a couple of weeks, he'd be useless, the police in the form of Wilkinson would be hanging around and - but he didn't say anything except,

"If that's what you want Hine, then it's just what I want." She kissed him and said goodnight.

Rewi and Golly came to pick Paul up in the Mark II on a Wednesday about ten days after he'd gone into hospital. They'd taken the day off work and Paul felt so good to be with them, especially to be on the right side of Golly again. He was still weak and had to go to the hospital every day for a couple of weeks to have his wrists re-bandaged. He still couldn't do much, but it was fine to be riding around in the back of the car, the fresh air blowing on his face and through his hair. On the way home they drove through the city. Paul thought how it was good to see people walking around and just everyday life going on, compared to the invalids and sickness which had been my companion for the last week and a half.

They went straight home to Ponsonby and Paul got into Hine's bed, exhausted. Hone brought him a cup of tea and he fell asleep in a few minutes. After a couple of hours Hone came in and they talked. Paul Calvert felt stronger and as they sat having their kōrero it seemed like a dream that he'd been in hospital at all, although the pain which flashed through his wrists every now and then served as a reminder that it was all real enough.

Calvert listened intently as Golly related the events of the Saturday and Sunday whilst he had been detained. About midnight on the night he was abducted, Hone had got a call from Eggars warning him that the cops were on their way round. They had been to Rewi and Liz's place and turned it upside down because they thought that Calvert had been involved with Johnson whom Wilkinson had suspected of being involved in some kind of dirty work. When the inspector found out from Eggars that there had been a third man he was convinced there was some kind of conspiracy

"They knew you had been stayin' here sometimes, so they came runnin'. Fortunately, Hine, she was up North, eh, seein' our Kuia – she'd been pretty upset over you still during those weeks since you had your bust-up!" At this Paul Calvert felt a mixture of guilt and relief. She had been thinking of him and missing him, as he had her!

"Anyway," Hone went on, "the pigs arrived and they bloody wrecked the place, they thought theys really on to something - they kept saying they knew who I was, and they knew who you were, this was the end of the road, all this sort of shit! Skids was stayin' that night and he was completely bemused by the whole thing, not least of all because they didn't even say anything to him, they left him alone. He just sat around laughing and making jokes while they picked on his older brother for a change."

Here Golly stopped to answer the phone. Calvert just sat there propped up in bed waiting for Golly's story to continue. He was thinking how different his life was after only a month back in Auckland after the long, indolent, beautiful years of sorrow and joy and discovery in dreamland...we spent the whole week preparing the hangi in te wahi moemoeä...one day we dug the pit, the next day we gathered the wood...instead of river stones we used the more traditional railway iron, small chunks of rail, fish-plates and the like...we made the journey from Parimoana into the city markets where we got our hua whenua and our hua räkau - our vegetables and fruit...we got a lot of meat and several pigs' heads, one of which was put on top of the Zombie Kombi, so that we drove back home with our poaka on high through the late evening mist past the Wharemanuka down on to the flat marshland - past the Hard Rock Cafe, and then we climbed up the hills and over the railway crossings until we reached the gates of Parimoana...because I was the 'Rangatira o Parimoana' it was my duty to christen Lady Rose's new baby...after the hangi around the night-fire outside our whare I gave her baby the new name and mana to enter the world...so it goes in Parimoana, te wahi moemoeä o te tonga..."That was Sis on the phone," said Hone coming back into the room. " She wanted to know how you are. She said she'll be home in about an hour or something. She's gonna get us a kai on her way home". Then Hone continued his re-telling of events.

"Anyway, what was really weird about this cop was he kept saying to me, 'You're Mr. Polynesia, aren't you - we know all about you!' It was real funny at first. Skids and I just cracked up laughing eh, every time he said Mr fucking Polynesia - it sounded so funny! But then, old Wilks got serious. He slammed me up against the wall, he was like a man possessed. 'You're Mr Polynesia, head of an international drug ring supplying heroin to the Pacific Basin. You were an off-shoot of the Mr Asia bastards, we've got an identikit picture of you back at the station - very clever of you to slum it in a run down part of Ponsonby rather than living the international high-life of your predecessors. But we've got you now Polynesia!' He pushed me violently against the wall again - I was completely confused, eh Paul."

Calvert was laughing. It seemed so funny thinking of Hone being a big time dealer.

"It was weird," said Hone. "He took me down to Auckland Central - Skids came along for the ride - and he interrogated me, he really thought he had a big fish, eh, but after a while inconsistencies came through in his idea of what I'd been up to and what I'd been doing. The final disproof came when he looked up that film thing with my criminal record on the Wanganui computer. When I was supposed to have been up in bloody Thailand setting up a big deal I was actually doing a stretch in Mt. Eden for aggravated robbery when I was still with the Blacks! First time I been glad to have a criminal record, eh!"

Apparently from then on Wilkinson and Hone got on really well, as they and Skids concentrated on finding Paul Calvert. It was actually Skids who came up with the idea of looking in the wool-store area. A few years before when he was about twelve or so he had been in his first gang. They all used to roam around town and they would look for places to hide or have fights with other gangs. The area around The Strand and the back of the Railway Station was perfect, and for a long time they used the area as a battle ground and general hang-out. Until one time when things went wrong and Marion Cotton was killed at the Railway Station during one of those deserted nights. Since then the area had been regarded as tapu by the street gangs, but Skids thought it would be the perfect place.

"It was Monday morning by then," said Golly, "and having tried everything else, Wilco agreed it was a good idea. We went from building to building - it was a very bright, sunny day eh. When we found you it was strange - you were nearly dead Paul. We went into the office - the whole place was very dark - but we turned on the light, and it was weird. The whole office was done out with Nazi flags, swastikas, pictures of Hitler - it was crazy! There was a hypodermic syringe lying on the table and a Luger beside it just like in the fucken war comics. There was also a copy of that photo you showed old Blunt of your father - by the way Blunt rang, he wants you to contact him, eh."

At this point Hine arrived home so Hone and Paul stopped talking about all that stuff and Golly left them alone.

"You cook the kai, e brother," Hine called after him. Calvert thought it was strange that he didn't remember any of the Nazi paraphernalia that Hone talked about in the office except the uniforms, but he was pretty out-of-it at the time so it wasn't that unusual.

Anyway, he soon forgot all that trash when Hine started talking with him. They were very loving with each other and Paul thought how it had been worth it to go through all that loneliness and pain if it helped to bring them together again, and far more closely and affectionately this time. He knew that the real test would come when he resumed everyday life, that anyone could be nice and sympathetic to someone who was sick in bed. However, he felt they were laying the foundation for a good relationship and he knew she felt it too. He was tired so they had dinner and Hine, after watching TV for a while, came to bed early.

Paul's hands being bandaged the way they were made physical expression of their love somewhat difficult, but they were happy just to be close to each other and they talked and listened to music. Of course, Hine had to be up for work, so she put the light out about eleven. Calvert was still tired but didn't especially want to sleep, so he lay there in the dark with the woman he loved asleep beside him...I got off the sub-way car at West 4th Street, Washington Square Station, walked up a block of the Avenue of the Americas into Waverley Place where the hotel I was staying at was situated...the Hotel Earle was one of those moderately priced New York places which reminded me of Brooklyn Flats in Emily Place, only a lot better...I walked in the main door and headed towards the elevator..."Gotta note for ya, Mr. Calvert," the person who ran the Earle called across the foyer...I took the note from where he sat behind a large glass cage - all transactions being done through a small letter-box size slit in the glass..."Thanks," I said, and then walked away towards the elevator again, thinking about who could be sending me a personal note, when I didn't know anyone in New York...I was also thinking how that glass-cage arrangement wasn't unlike similar set-ups in some Auckland all-night gas stations...as I ruminated over the coming-of-age of my hometown I read the note: 'Meet us at One, at the third park bench from the right on the university side of Washington Square - signed H.V.K., R.O'H., & M.C'...I made my way through Washington Square to the far side where New York University's older buildings fronted onto the park...as I tried to decipher the hieroglyphics of the initials of whoever had signed the note I caught odd glimpses of the oddest people...Washington Square was a hang-out right at the end of Fifth Avenue and more or less marked the beginning of Greenwich Village...it was a very mixed area with some of those fine New York apartments, and not far away North of 14th Street things started to deteriorate...I was walking across the square, and cops were cruising around in what were meant to be walkways on the look-out for anything when a tall, black cat came up to me out-of-it on something and said, "Man! wanna check out some fistin', check it out man." I declined his magnanimous gesture (It's a good thing I didn't answer him with the proverbial New York comeback jive, "All right, get down, gimme five!")...when I approached the park bench I could hardly believe what I saw...there were three old people, two men and a woman in their seventies, I suppose, all sitting talking quietly to each other like old friends...when they saw me I heard the woman cry out "here he comes!"...it was an extraordinary scene in that New York park, one of the men was dressed in an SS Colonels uniform, the other had a black beret, black skivvy and trousers and dark glasses, the 'uniform' of the I.R.A., and the woman was in green, with a long pleated skirt like an Irish colleen, but around her head she wore a tipare with the feather of a huia...I was overcome with emotion and astonishment to see my two fathers and my mother sitting there talking away to each other and my mother calling "Haere mai, e tama. Come on, son, come over here"...it was crazy and the sun shone in my eyes, white light filled my mind, I was dizzy..."Wake up, What's wrong, Paul! e Paul wake up!" Hine's voice came to him and Calvert felt strange as the light from the lamp shone in his eyes.

He was distraught, he didn't know what was going on, but Hine gradually brought his wairua mate, his sick spirit, back from the night with her aroha. As Paul told her of his dream she listened carefully - he was so glad she was with him, that he had her to tell these nightmares of his mind to. She responded by being very tender and loving and he felt like crying and crying because she was so beautiful.

The days of Paul Calvert's recuperation rolled by. It was about a month before he could use his hands and arms with any confidence. He had been in touch with Tony Blunt who again had something of interest for him. Blunt laughed when he heard Hine and Paul were together again.

"The eighth wonder of the world, eh Calvert, human relationships! I hope you'll be more civilised next time you come for dinner - or have you two developed your little act into something of a party trick? Seriously old man, why don't you and Hine come around on Monday night for dinner, and we'll have a chat about this latest stuff I've uncovered - only this time be good enough to tell Hine about what we've got to say!"

Paul promised him he would and added that even he didn't know what it was about this time.

"True enough," said Blunt with a chuckle, "Well, till Monday!"

On the Saturday before they were due to go to the Blunts, Inspector Wilkinson came around and wanted to talk to him. Apparently, they'd found another Nazi's nest done out in a similar fashion to the wool-store. They had raided an address in Balmoral hoping to find drugs. When they got there, the cops found a printing press and piles of pamphlets of an inflammatory neo-Nazi type. There was also a quantity of heroin and other drugs, but no trace of people. But there was one curious detail that almost escaped their attention.

A copy of the German magazine 'Der Speigel' lay open on the floor. The page it was open on had an article about SS members still on the run, and on the opposite page was a photograph of Helmut von Klagen and a little feature story. The story alleged that Paul's father had escaped after the war with the plans to set up a new Reich, and that he knew where billions of dollars worth of gold were, set aside to carry out such a rejuvenation of the Nazi State. Paul Calvert wondered on this for the next day or so. He got out the photograph in question and looked at it again and again, trying to figure out what there was about it that made it so sought after. It seemed to have no secret attachments or hidden back or the like. He kept looking for clandestine words or numbers in the background but there appeared to be none.

Wilkinson too, had had it examined thoroughly when Calvert had brought the picture back from Manurewa but even the police experts could find nothing unusual about it. By Sunday evening Paul felt he had exhausted every possibility of finding solutions for the mystery. He was tired and went to bed early and read. Hine went to bed after the Sunday horror movie which was 'really neat' apparently. Although Paul was tired he felt in a playful mood, so when she was settled in bed, he said to her:

"Hine, you know the doctor said I have to exercise my fingers."

She said "ai" as he opened and closed my hands slowly, accentuating the movements. She looked puzzled as he then asked her:

"How's your geography of the Bay of Plenty?" Totally bemused she said "What?" Paul waited for a minute or so savouring her feeling of mystery then he said, completely deadpan,

"I'll teach you a trick that an Māori old lady told me about when I was in Kawhia once! It will increase your knowledge of the Bay of Plenty and will send my fingers out for exercise all at once."

He heard her mutter "bloody porangi" but she fell silent when he asked her,

"How far is it from Te Puke to Te Teko?" He said it in a way that sounded as though the words were running into one another, yet she could still hear what he was saying. Hinengaro said she didn't know how far it was from bloody Te Puke to bloody Te Teko. "Well," he said with amusement in his voice, "Well, the old kuia in the Kawhia pub told me the best way measure the distance is like this." He put his thumb gently on her belly and said, "That's where you start at 'te puku' and then you move slowly down through the beautiful bush-clad country," as he moved his fingers down her body he could feel the excitement rising in both of them, "and you keep down until you reach 'te teke' And that's how far it is."

They were both laughing and made love joyfully, and then laughed again and were very affectionate with each other.

"S'pose you tell that to all the girls," Hine said. Paul made a faint protest and they fell asleep restful and replete in each other's arms.

Hine was late for work the next morning, something which she hated. Paul was half asleep as she got ready, cursing and swearing all the while to the morning music of funky Z.M., loud but not so clear.

"See you at five, eh," she said as she kissed Paul good-bye and he was glad that she and all the noise were gone so he could go back to sleep and dream of her.

When he met Hine after work she was tired and irritable.

"Bloody bastards at work, they tell me off for being late, and made me work through lunch. How you, eh?" Paul told her he was fine, a little tired because this was his first time out really.

"But I'm glad to be out with you, Hine. Let's go and have a drink and then we'll get a taxi to Blunt's." She smiled and they kissed.

They left the bar where the Snakepit used to be and walked across the square to the taxi-rank opposite The Olde Customs House. Paul gave the driver the address and they headed into Quay Street and east out along the waterfront drive. Hine took Paul's hand and they sat enjoying the evening and being with each other...*I held tight to the bottle of whiskey I had stolen from the pub in te wahi moemoeä...I barely remember the journey home, and Paddy who was driving, doesn't remember at all...but there we were travelling down the winding turning port road at a rate of knots in the old World War II Chev truck singin' the rebel songs at the top of our voices, now and then sluggin' away on the Tullamore Dew...that's all I remember till the mornin' now, when I woke it was a terrible hangover, but I was alive and in my room with "Good-bye to Skibbereen" and "Peggy Gordon you are me darling" running around me own head...I looked out the window after blindin' me self pullin' back the curtains...beyond the old town, the dirty old town, the dog town of the port of te wahi moemoeä, where tall ships stood a hundred years ago bringing the seeds of the likes of us and ours, beyond this town lay the land which looked like a woman's body, stretched out in the form of a peninsula, breasts and things all in perfect proportion, nature emulating art emulating nature...my head reminded me of Paddy and the whiskey and the Chev which knew its own way home...I saw down at my desk to write a poem which began "I have been drunk!" and then I dreamed in te wahi moemoeä...*"That'll be $17.50 thanks," said the cab driver. Paul Calvert watched this yellow Falcon taxi drive off along the manicured street where Blunt lived. There seemed to be a lot more yellow cabs in Auckland these days and he thought to himself that while the Council and A.R.A. big-wigs were trying desperately to turn the

city into the L.A. of the South Pacific, with its corresponding lack of public transport and amenities, maybe the Auckland cab companies were trying to introduce the Big Apple influence. Maybe when the taxi company takes over the Council they will get a decent subway railway system to complement the Yellow Cabs, Calvert thought. His reverie was broken by Hine.

"We're here, Paul," she said.

"Where?" he replied. She looked at him in mock disgust and went on up the path. Paul heard Hinengaro laugh to herself as they walked past the fountain. It was strange that since the nightmarish heroin hallucinations he had begun subconsciously to think of Hine's name in its longer and more proper form.

"When you gonna prove your point, eh!" He too laughed as he remembered their discussion about the statue the last time we had been here. As he gave Hine a small slap on the bum, he noticed Blunt was standing on the verandah watching them.

"Getting ready for the big hit after dinner, are we?" Hine looked embarrassed and they both turned away.

"Come in Calvert, Hine," said Tony, "only joking!" Cara was waiting inside and greeted them both warmly, although a bit uncertainly.

"Lovely to see you both again," she said, smiling at Hine while casting a doubtful look in Paul's direction...*mum was making an apple pie and dad and I were out on the back porch where he was having a beer, and the radio was blaring with a Saturday afternoon rugby match interspersed with racing commentaries...*"I'll get this one" said dad quietly as he picked up the empty beer bottle...his arm moved back over his head in a slow motion and then quick like an arrow let the bottle fly, the bottle flew off in one direction as it hit the ground and the rat which he had tried to hit ran off the opposite way..."Bastard!" cried dad. It was great fun when dad stayed home with us on a Saturday afternoon. "Here, Paul, you have the next go!"...dad handed me a beer bottle...as I waited for the inevitable rat to appear I could smell the smells of domestic industry...the apple pie smell of cloves and fresh apples and pastry in one nostril and in the other the smell of washing and smoke as the copper washed our clothes - I used to love getting the copper ready, lighting the fire after the wood had been chopped...boy, I was happy, as I let the bottle fly...*"Hope, you have been listening to me, Calvert!" said Tony. Paul looked up and there was my old friend from university days, Tony Blunt - it seemed unreal, maybe it was just a trick of the mind.

"Oh! I'm sorry Tony I must have been dreaming!"

"Anyway, let's go to dinner, you two are always late!" Blunt said mischievously.

Dinner was delicious and the wines were of the best foreign vintage. Soon after they had all finished eating the two women, obviously pleased to see each other, excused themselves from the table and went off to have a talk. This left Tony and Paul sitting in the big dining room together. Blunt poured them both a large cognac and suggested they might go into the library. It was a strange feeling that Paul Calvert got from this house, everything was so in order, so perfect.

No children or pets running around, no hint of the general chaos of life. Paul thought of Liz and Rewi and their constant struggle to make ends meet and to even keep their house in some order; and here were the Blunts living in an almost supernatural circumstance, with nothing but their own existences to impinge upon this serenity. Paul wondered how often they felt like smashing all their china and crystal, or how often they felt like taking to each other with machetes. "We just don't talk," he remembered Blunt had said of their way of arguing the night he'd hit Hine.

"Well Calvert," said Blunt as they were both seated in the dark, wood-paneled room surrounded on three sides by volumes of books, which in the main were leather-bound and law related. There was also a large collection of first editions and the overall effect of this library was like being on a BBC production set in one of those rooms from a scene in one of Dickens' classic tales.

"Well Calvert, this little caper of your family is quite beginning to take over my pre-occupation. It is actually very interesting from a legal as well as an historical standpoint. This recent discovery of mine, whilst still somewhat in the realm of conjecture, is nonetheless altogether feasible and will just need the addition of a few further facts for verification." At this Blunt took a large drink from his brandy glass and excused himself from the room.

A short while later he returned with a newly opened bottle of Cognac and two old-looking books. One was 'Ao-tea-roa' by William Pember Reeves, an early New Zealand poet, politician and commentator. But it was the second book which made Paul Calvert give out an almost hysterical yelp of laughter! If it wasn't so old, he should have thought Tony had put it together as some kind of elaborate joke. When Paul had recovered himself, with the aid of a large gulp of that refined brandy, he looked at the title of the book again. 'The Aryan Maori', by Edward Tregear, published in 1885 by George Didsbury, Government Printer. It was too much! He didn't know how to react.

On the one hand he felt "So what?" - some eccentric Nineteenth Century philologist obsessed with the world making sense, had come up with a theory about the Māori people being of Aryan origin. On the other hand, the absurd notion that all this may have something to do with his parents disturbed him. He decided to have another Cognac and listen to what Blunt had to say.

"I was just flicking through Pember Reeves", Blunt began. "I like to read him now and then for his interesting angle on New Zealand's development – he's our only Poet-Statesman, which is interesting in itself. In the chapter headed 'The Māori' he discusses, among other things, the origin of the indigenous people. Having dismissed any connection with Asians or the aborigines of Australia, or American or Mexican Indians, he comes to this phrase -" here Tony opened the book at Page 34 and pointed to a sentence 'They are much more like some of the Aryans of Northern India.'

Blunt continued, "While unremarkable in itself, because Pember Reeves goes on to say that the Māori are firmly Polynesian in origin, it did remind me of a book that I once picked up cheaply as a curiosity. So I looked through the bookshelf until I found Tregear's book, which I had never read. When I read the introductory chapter, which begins with a quote from a German thinker from the period who writes of 'The discovery of a new world...' and relates it to the birth of Philology. And later on when Tregear talks of the Nagas from the Poetry of Sanskrit whose king, Anat, is said to have had a thousand hooked heads, on each of which was the 'Swastika,' the mystic cross, it was a bit strange. Together with what you've told me Paul, about von Klagen, from what I've found out about him and his Nazi connection and with this weird chap Tregear's theories about the Māori being Aryan, my mind was awash with ideas..."

At this point Cara announced coffee, which Blunt and Calvert declined. Cara and Hinengaro both came into the library then and told us that we were both rude pigs and that they were going downtown to a nightclub to enjoy themselves. The men's protests and attempted explanation fell on deaf ears, and as Tony tossed Cara the keys of the Mercedes his final words of 'drive carefully' received a very disdainful look indeed! But they both left chattering and laughing, and Blunt and Calvert concluded that things weren't too bad.

"We now enter the realm of pure conjecture," said Tony, and they soon forgot the women as they both became transfixed by what Blunt was saying. It was like one of those 'once upon a time' stories of childhood, except that this was a fairy tale about Paul Calvert's own past, strange and wonderful and quite frightening. Blunt continued,

"Now, let's pretend you are von Klagen sitting in your research office at a German University in 1938 trying to dream up theories of Aryan superiority. You've got unlimited funding and time to purchase and read every book or paper on the subject."

It all became rather eerie for Calvert as the mixture of brandy and Tony's story began to take effect on his mind - there was only one thing for it, more cognac and more story!

Blunt continued. "One day, you, von Klagen, come across a reference to Edward Tregear's 'The Aryan Maori' and immediately you're hooked - an entirely new tack. So, you somehow get hold of a copy and as soon as you read it you see a reference to swastikas and you're away. At this point, Calvert, we have to assume your long time assertion that your mother had Māori blood has some truth in it."

"Go on," Paul said as he sat in this deliberately antiquated room letting Tony's words waft around him, like some zombie sitting in a swirling mist. It all sounded so plausible, well, as authentic as any of the other realities which had happened to him since he'd returned from dreamland. It was funny how reality seemed so much more real in dreamland - now, here he was in the real world where so many fanciful and nightmarish things had happened in the last month or so. So much had his mind slipped its moorings that now Blunt's conjecture seemed irrefutable, almost palpable - Paul felt that perhaps he was having heroin's equivalent of an LSD flash-back. His feelings and thoughts were all so jumbled that he could not answer the question 'do I wake or sleep?' with any accuracy. However, as he saw Blunt replenishing their glasses and heard his charming, inquisitive voice he knew things to be real enough.

"Now, enter Richard Calvert," Blunt continued, "von Klagen's contact with the I.R.A., to whom he's selling arms and ammunition on behalf of the Nazi Government. I'll no longer act as though you are von Klagen, but move fully into the third person," Blunt says to Calvert as he begins to relish the feel of the English language in an almost Irish way. Paul thanks him and he moves on.

"During one of Calvert's visits to Germany under the guise of being a university scholar he happens to mention to von Klagen that he has lived in New Zealand and that he has a New Zealand fiancé, your mother! During a somewhat drunken conversation, Calvert mentions that this girl has some native blood in her, and von Klagen is ecstatic. How he would like to mate with her and produce another strain of Aryan..."

"Enough!" Paul cries out like a wounded animal. "Are you suggesting that I am alive because of some perverted fucking SS experiment into genetic purity?" The thought of this horrifies him and he cannot speak. He feels morbid and crestfallen. His whole existence appears before him as a monstrous joke, but one which sickens him rather than makes me laugh.

"Now, take it easy, old boy. Was it Augustine who said we must love our children, even those conceived in lust. Well, surely the same goes for our parents, even those who conceive us in experiments." Paul Calvert tried hard to be dismissive about Blunt's witticism, but in the end he laughed, not because what Blunt said was funny, but more because there was nothing else he could do, other than cry. So Blunt and Calvert talked, discussed, argued, and got drunk for the next few hours.

The next morning Paul woke up with the sun in my eyes, barely able to move. He didn't recognise anything, even when he could see through his dazed haze of a hangover.

Hine and Calvert were both sprawled haphazard over a large bed and she was still asleep. They both were fully clothed and still had their shoes on. Paul had never seen this room before and it looked unlike any place he had previously slept in. It resembled a very plush-expensive hotel rather than someone's house. There was a small chandelier in the middle of the ceiling and everything in the room except Paul and Hine was so neat and in order. On the walls were some tasteful prints, an original Illingworth, and a couple of charcoal sketches by McCahon from the 'Jet Out' series. Paul lay there between dreams and sleep and Cognac ambience and Hine slept there beside him in her own dreams. He felt complete and almost unworldly, as though they had left the earth together and were travelling on a thought of what the world should be like.

"Breakfast, dears!" Cara's voice broke the morning like the ray of sunlight when Calvert had first opened his eyes. Cara and Tony entered the guest room with trays of fruit and cereal, milk, coffee and other more exotic food, if they felt more inclined towards 'that kind of thing'.

"What's the time, Paul, where are we?" Paul heard Hine half groan from her side of the bed. "I'll be late for work."

"I've taken care of that dear," said Cara, "I rang them and said you're not well."

Hine, who never missed a day's work, began to protest but soon gave up. The four of them sat around the bed, eating at leisure and talking quietly about anything that wasn't too heavy. The Blunts even suggested that Hine and Calvert should come and live there with them, and as they looked out across Orakei Basin, down the Hauraki Gulf, on that lovely morning it seemed like a really good idea.

Hine was enjoying what was probably the first taste of affluence in her life, and when she turned and said "shall we Paul?" She looked almost ecstatic and Calvert felt for a moment that they might. They all joked and laughed and carried on for quite some time. It was midday before Tony said, "Oh! It's time I got going, I have to be at the office in half an hour, damn it!"

At that point Paul Calvert remembered last night's conversation with Blunt. A dark cloud moved across the East Auckland sky and as the sky got blacker so did his thoughts. Hine and Paul accepted a lift into town with Tony. Calvert sat silent and moody in the back while Hine and Tony talked away in the front of the Mercedes. No one had noticed Paul's change in mood and he was pleased. Earlier Cara had said, "You're quiet all of a sudden, Paul." He said he was just tired and everyone left it at that, but when Blunt dropped them off at the bottom of Kitchener Street near the court, Hine knew straight away that something was wrong.

Paul felt reluctant to talk, but she pressed me so they went into 'Cafe by the Park', ordered lunch and talked all afternoon until the manager closed the restaurant. Paul told Hine all about the Aryan Māori thing and of Blunt's conjectures and conclusions. He told her he felt tainted by the knowledge that he may be the living result of a racial experiment. He said that he had always felt guilty about being alive, but attributed that to his Catholic upbringing with its emphasis on the darker side of things, rather than any palpable sin or fault.

After talking for a long time the Cognac after-effect was moving languidly through his body and Paul Calvert felt that he might just disappear or evaporate if he spoke any more. He also felt the heroin horror of his neo-Nazi captivity returning in his mind. He was adrift in a sea of grey night moves and Hine, sitting beside him, was the only light in a life of shadows.

Hine steered the conversation back to an easier level. "Cara and I had quite a good time last night, e." They had been night-clubbing, and Cara had paid all night so they went to all the good clubs.

"One place we went to was weird, boy! Only women allowed - they're all lesbians and that. I didn't think much of it e, but that Cara was right into it. We were pretty out of it by then and she was kissing all these types and that. I think she knew them all, like she went there all the time or something. And these real butch women kept coming up to me, saying things like 'You must be Cara's new girlfriend - took her long enough to get a Māori!' and things like that. But the music was good and Cara was buying drinks and I felt alright - it was pretty weird though e, Paul."

The next few weeks went past without incident. With the exception of the odd brooding moments over what had surfaced about his life Paul Calvert was quite happy. Hine and he became closer and closer and Paul felt at last he had met a woman with whom he could share his life. He no longer dreamed, because reality was now bearable. Although at times when he thought about his shattered past and the things he had recently learned about his parents since arriving back in Auckland, he became anxious and confused, the number of times he actually thought about all that stuff decreased. He was living more in the present. He had returned to work, and that made him feel stronger, not only physically but also because he was earning a full wage again so that he was more emotionally and materially secure.

Paul Calvert began to appreciate Auckland as a place as he became less sensitive to the bad experience he had had both in the near and distant past. On weekends Hinengaro and he would go for long walks around different parts of the city. Sometimes they would catch a bus, any bus, to the end of its route and walk for miles to the end of another route where they'd get that bus back to the city. Also, at this time they saw a lot of Liz and Rewi. Liz was well advanced by now and Hine liked going out and giving her a hand with the other kids while Rewi and Paul would be off in the car to get a kai, seafood, fish or just doing things around their house. Eggars was often away these days giving poetry readings around the country. He was becoming something of a celebrity and his writing career was really developing.

CHAPTER 6

One Friday night Paul got home from work quite late. They had been mending a burst sewer pipe and he was up to his neck in shit and mud. It had been a really hot day and he felt exhausted, sweaty and in a bad mood because he had cut his finger on a piece of old pipe and had to go to the doctor to get a tetanus shot.

"Where you been?" said Hine.

"Where the fuck do you think I've been!" Paul replied. She looked hurt, so he calmed down and told her of his day over a cup of tea. Golly came into the kitchen, having got home earlier.

"There's a telegram for you, e hoa."

He handed it to Paul, and Hine and he went on talking as he opened it. At first Calvert couldn't understand a word of what he read. He showed it to Hine and Golly then he looked at it again.

"Meet me in Aotea Square at 1p.m. tomorrow - STOP - it is urgent - STOP - I will be on the third seat from the right by the Town Hall - STOP - V.K."

He couldn't work it out at all, but then Hine remembered the dream he had told her about meeting his parents at Washington Square in New York. At first Paul thought it was an absurd connection, but the more he thought about it the more it made sense. And it was signed with the initials V.K. - Von Klagen! Paul couldn't believe it.

"Prepare to meet your maker," quipped Golly.

The telegram, however, was not the only surprise that evening. Calvert rang Wilkinson to tell him of the telegram and the cop said he'd be around straight away. Paul Calvert was tired and after dinner he sat in an armchair just letting his thoughts float through his mind about his father. 'What would he be like? What would I feel? What would I say to him?' He felt curious more than condemnatory. It was so strange and seemed quite unrelated to reality. Paul had noticed throughout the evening how quiet Hine was as Hone and he discussed the prospect of a long summer, and where they should go for their holidays.

"We got two weeks off, e," said Hone. "We should go up north and see our whanau, e sis. Mum and dad are goin' up to the Marae with Skids and Te Arohanui." Hine nodded silently - she seemed overwhelmed by something. Paul looked at her. She went to look away, but then said, "Come into our room, Paul." She said it with such an eerie, almost ethereal voice it cast him in a kind of a spell. When she stood up she seemed to glide out of the living-room. Paul Calvert followed as if in a trance.

"Kei te hapu ahau," she said gently. It was the first time Hine had spoken to him in Māori. The fact that she told him she was pregnant was made that more poignant by the strength of hearing her speak her own language. Paul was almost crying, she was so beautiful and now their lives would be entwined forever by a child. This is what he felt, but he reacted quite differently, almost as though he were two people.

"What do you mean you're fucking pregnant!" Hine recoiled from his anger. "Why didn't you tell me - weren't you using any fucking contraceptives, you stupid...!"

"Were you?" came her defiant retort, and they both fell quiet.

"What's going on?" Golly yelled from the door, fearful that Calvert may have attacked his sister again.

"I'm all right brother!" Hine called back to him. "I'll tell you later."

Paul Calvert sat there on the edge of the bed not knowing where to look or how to react. Hine had been right to throw it back at him, to force him to think about his responsibility. He knew that there would be no long discussion, no lengthy analysis of why, what and wherefore, it was not her way. Here was a fact of life that had to be dealt with. That's why she had told him in Māori. She knew that that was part of her strength in their relationship, and that he would respond more honestly and emotionally out of his feeling for that aspect of life. What Paul had told her about Tania and Melissa had obviously taught her a lot about him.

She knew that his respect for te reo and te taha Māori was tied up in his mind with the female element of life – ngā wahine toa! She knew that Rangi had been the catalyst for this to emerge, that he had thought of Rangi as having the mana of pounamu and that she had been precious and hidden and thus unattainable to him. Hine had made sure of all this and had quietly worked out for herself how to know him better than he did himself.

The way Calvert knew himself was through self-doubt and confused thoughts and dreams about life. But Hinengaro knew his strengths and had waited until she had needed him to use her power which came from this knowledge. However, Calvert's old self fought back, and he came out with all the old arguments. 'Where would we live? How would we get by financially? Would the child, like me, be tainted by the sins of my past generations? Might it even be deformed because of unknown genetic experiments. What kind of world were we bringing a child into-unemployment, nuclear wars?'

All the old rational arguments came out, but there was a life in Hine's womb which defied all reason. She knew this, and as each of his arguments tramped their weary way from his mind to his mouth where they evaporated from being into nothingness, he too began to know Hine's quiet joy.

There he was crying and laughing once all his thoughts had finished and he let go. He kissed and hugged Hine and they were both together in happiness and in sorrow, in sickness and in health. He was no longer alone with only his own mohio porangi for solace. It was crazy and simple and was he no longer needed to justify his existence to anyone. He was alive and he had created life just like the Hebrew God, except that he had needed someone else to make him whole. Whereas the Lord had created male and female out of the void, the Lord being of both elements, he being of only one of those elements, had to find the other half struggling through the void of his own mind.

In the process he had stumbled through dreams and illusions like a wild animal, trampling on anything in his path. But that was not the way he had learned from Rangi, from Tania, from Miranda, from Aroha, from anyone he had tried to force to love him. Hine and Paul kissed tenderly and passionately, and he always kept this evening in mind when future times of trouble and torment dogged their relationship.

They went out into the living room and told Golly the news. He was really happy - it would be his first niece or nephew!

"Or maybe both, eh!" Paul threw something at him. The sun was just about out of the sky. Through the window, out beyond Te Puke o Wairaka and the Western Suburbs, they caught a glimpse of the last stages of the Waitakere sunset. The sky lit up crimson, as the sun disappeared behind the ranges in a final show against the all embracing darkness. There was almost a violence in the beauty, as though the sky was empathising with some hidden struggle that was going on in the human heart.

Wilkinson arrived about eight thirty, and as they passed through the social niceties into the matter at hand, Paul realised why the cop and Golly had got on so well. Wilkinson was a tall man with abrupt manners, but he really listened to what people said and appreciated anyone who talked their mind. Calvert imagined the hard time the cop had given Golly when he thought he was Mr Polynesia, because he had a genuine hatred of hard drugs and those who peddled them. His own daughter had died of an overdose a few years before, and he was convinced that drug and alcohol addiction were the true social ills of the time.

"By the way, Golly, we found Polynesia," Wilkinson said during their conversation about Calvert's father, "or should I say the American Coast Guard found his body off the New England coast. He was riddled with bullets and was only found because a trawler caught his weighted body in a net. I'm considering getting some compensation for you because of the false arrest I made of you!"

Hone thanked him and then Wilko said, "You realise we'll have to arrest your father Calvert, when you meet him tomorrow. He's still wanted by the West Germans to face war crimes charges. I've informed Interpol on the matter and they're sending a couple of chaps over to start extradition proceedings."

Of course Paul Calvert hadn't realised or thought about this aspect, and had only informed the police in case the neo-Nazi group tried to capture or kill his father. So he had betrayed he own father even before he even met him. He was a Judas now, whereas before he was the God of Israel.

"Can I spend a while talking to him before you take him?" Wilkinson agreed to 'about ten minutes'

"Phone for you Inspector, Hine announced from the hall. Wilkinson left the room and Paul plunged into a feeling of remorse and self-hatred.

"You weren't to know," said Hine, trying to comfort me.

"I've got to go immediately," said the policeman. "Stay away from town tonight," he added and walked out the door.

"I'll go to the Gluepot and get some beer to celebrate your baby," said Hone. Hine and Paul sat watching TV and talking. It was now dark and Calvert felt it inside him. It seemed like the middle of winter when everything is cold and dead, but their baby was already the first flower of spring in his mind, delicate and vulnerable and full of promise. This is what he had wanted Hine for, he thought, to stop the endless merry-go-round of relationships and emptiness, pain and numbness.

Now it would be permanent, as permanent as life could be. He also realised that this is what Hine had wanted from him. That is why she had come back and why she was pregnant. He supposed that her visit up north, when she went to see her kuia who had persuaded her to take on her full Māori name, Hinengaro Te Riro i He, had something to do with her decision to return to him. He was about to ask her about that when Golly came in with a dozen beer followed closely by Skids.

"Hurry up, shut the door, man." Hone urged, there was an air of urgency and excitement about their talk and action.

"Fuckin' cops!" Skids spat it out like a bitter taste. As Paul Calvert saw blood trickling down his face onto Skid's shirt, and his hair matted and turned red, he felt almost sick. Hine went up to her younger brother and was about to take him by the hand to the bathroom and clean him up when she stopped short.

"Where'd you get this?" She pointed to a solid gold chain which hung around his neck, and Paul also noticed that he wore a couple of very expensive rings on his fingers

"Down Queen Street, man, It's all happening - riots eh! Everyone's breaking windows and taking what they want. They're throwing things at the cops, it's the real thing!"

Suddenly, whack! Hine gave him a backhander and Skids fell on to the floor, knocking over the table with the beer on it. He cowered before her as she threatened to hit him again,

"You rotten little thief!" she screamed. "You little bastard, all the bloody men in the family are the same - nothing but trouble. Your bloody brother and your father, they always been in trouble - fucking gangs or the R.S.A. or whatever. I can't even go home to see mum most of the time because dad's always drunk and he beats her and he beats me too if I'm around! Mum and I have tried to bring some respect to the family - we always had jobs, not like you mangere – all those times I had to stay off school just to look after you lot while mum was working cause dad was too boozed to get a job."

She picked up a bottle of beer and smashed it on the side of the crate.

"I hate this stuff and I hate you!" she screeched and waved the broken bottle close to Skid's face.

"No wonder Rina went to Wellington as soon as she could. Just because a bunch of stupid porangi bloody idiots go looting and rioting on a Friday night doesn't mean you have to – haven't you got any brains, e – I suppose you find it all fucking funny do you?"

She then turned on Golly – "Well, you better wake up too, boy. Skids has followed your example and it won't be more than a few years before he's in some jail for shooting or raping or robbing someone. I s'pose you think that'll increase his great fucking mana, e! He'll be a big man then won't he?"

Hine put down the broken glass bottle and walked to the bedroom.

She turned before going in and said,

"Don't come in for a while Paul!" and she disappeared. She seemed calm now and almost happy. None of the men left in the room spoke or moved for a long time. Skids was crying quietly and looked like the small, frightened boy that he was. Golly was silent and when Paul looked at him he turned his head away.

The TV was on in the background and when the film finished there was a special newscast. There it was, Calvert turned up the sound, and watched and listened with a kind of awe. Riots in Auckland's main street. Ordinary cops and the riot squad all out there battering and being battered. Running battles, windows smashed and shops looted. Skids sat up, getting excited. He pointed to various scenes he had been in while keeping one eye on Hine's door to see if she would emerge and give him another crack over the head. As Police Head Perry was talking about the situation, one reporter asked what was going to be a provocative question implicating the police as instigators of the riot. The screen went blank and the sound fizzled.

"Fucking cops! said Golly, and Paul thought how his attitude epitomised a general attitude prevalent in this country among a large section of the community.

Paul Calvert supposed this to be an anti-police riot as much as anything. How apt the name 'riot squad' was! Since they first appeared at the Springbok demonstrations a few years before they had been nothing but a signal to riot. Their long batons, shields and Nazi type helmets were red rag to a bull. After half a minute or so the image of Perry, having sorted out who could say what, came back into the living room.

Paul remembered something the poet James k. Baxter had said a decade before, warning that if this man became a top Auckland policeman there would be trouble. Then there were more scenes from the streets, all sorts of people throwing all sorts of things. There had been a rock concert in Aotea Square, too much drink, too many drugs, too much of a good time. The police tried to arrest some people and bang! Everyone with something on their mind or some axe to grind exploded. Cars were turned over and set alight.

The large glass bars of the Queen Street barons became favourite targets for those who liked to smash things - provocative to display such affluence in times of unemployment and hardship! A lot of people would say that this was a race riot, that Māori and Polynesian kids had had enough. But it didn't have that feeling for Paul - it was just what happens when freedom is exercised by those who have never known how to use it This country had lived by a kind of unspoken repression through its education and other institutions for so long. Even those edifices which keep people alive such as Social Welfare invoke dissension. No one likes to feel constantly beholden to the hydra, the many-headed monster of myth and reality.

As the newscast finished Calvert felt very sad for his city – he had grown up here and he loved it. It had gone from a large overgrown country town to become a small big city and nobody had seen it happen. It was like finding out that your teenage daughter had been sleeping around while you thought she was at a friend's house. To use an academic phrase – Auckland had arrived! Watching all the tension and excitement on TV had broken the tension created by Hine. Golly and Skids and Paul sat around drinking the beer and talking about what had happened.

"This city's right for everything except people, man" said Golly. "It's right for cars, it's right for multi-million dollar buildings, it's right for tourists - but for people that live here, unless you're some middle-class, or white trash, or a cop, then you can't move."

The arguments went back and forth. Skids told them how he'd thrown a rubbish tin through Social Welfare's window in Wakefield Street and they laughed, though felt sad. Paul was happy and he was sad. He was happy to know that in the other room Hine lay asleep with their baby inside her – he felt the optimism one instinctively feels for a new generation. But he was sad for this city, or five cities or however many cities they thought there were. The only thing bringing them together was the motorways of the National Roads Board. It was absurd! And it seemed the people were clawing at each other too. It went back a long way. This city was built on misunderstanding. Things had never gone its way. It was acquired by Hobson to be a capital – that didn't last long. It grew haphazardly and was the toy of the Päkehä capitalists who had no respect for anything but money.

Now it was like a heavy undertow or rip at Piha. Auckland was built on several volcanoes and that night a social volcano had erupted. It was a long time coming and everyone would blame the fire and lava and say they never heard the rumblings, never looked below the surface for the seismic warnings which had been sending small tremors and quakes from the beginning.

Anything from the revered Päkehä–Mäori F.E. Manning, an early notary, saying in 1873 about education in the region, "I have nothing to report except that if all your schools are going as well as that of Wirinake there will soon be no Maoris in New Zealand," to the burning of the Orakei village, to the dawn raid on islanders in the early seventies, to the opening out and expansion of people's power in the Vietnam War and lately the Springbok demonstrations. These were tremors, violent or small, but the riot was an explosion! An eruption, small, but intense and it gave everyone a jolt. They kept talking and arguing to and fro. They talked about the '51 lockout and the Queen Street riots of the thirties, things Skids had never heard of.

Calvert said that that night's were different because they had been organised as an entertainment for people to enjoy themselves, and therefore it was an expression of an underlying frustration and hopelessness. The bands were all singing about nuclear war and unemployment, even days in the Amazon were a bore. People getting drunk and out of it, and thinking 'what the fuck, let's go for it' and it's all on. Golly thought Paul was a bit of a stooge.

"You think too much, man! Drink, don't think, Professor!" and he handed him another bottle. But Calvert kept on saying the riots of the thirties were directed at far more specific grievances. It was about two when Paul went to bed. Hine was asleep, but woke up when he got in beside her.

"You all right?" she said. He said he was and when she answered his questions about how she felt she confirmed what he thought. She felt great, she'd wanted to do that to one of her male family for years, but they'd all been too big. She said she was sorry that it may have upset him. They lay there in each other's arms with the radio on softly. "Kiss me, honey, honey kiss me" went an old song, as the radio waves infused themselves into their minds and came out as "Kiss me honihoni, kiss me!" They both laughed as they accentuated the Mäori words. Then they made love and went to sleep...dad was in prison...I watched as one of the last Sunderland Flying Boats turned slowly in the sky over Bastion Point...this was a day when things changed in Auckland forever...

friends of the family came to cut down the five large pohutukawa trees which adorned the steep slope of our front section...it was like close friends dying beside you in a war...Paul slept long that night and often dreamed of things he'd loved about Auckland that were now lost. When Hine woke him about ten for breakfast he felt he didn't know where he was. The two brothers and one sister had been up early and cleaned the house. Golly had cooked the kai and Paul knew that all our lives were bound together as whänau from now on.

At midday Paul kissed Hine good-bye and walked through Ponsonby towards the city to keep the appointment with his father, von Klagen. It was like walking in a dream, and as he made the descent from the top of Cook Street past the police Station into Aotea Square, he suddenly felt like a lost child. It was about ten to one as he hit the Square.

No-one was over by the Town Hall where his father said he'd meet him. Paul felt relieved – maybe he won't turn up – maybe he doesn't even exist. 'Perhaps I'm still in dreamland and, like Rangi and Tania and Miranda, he is simply what I think he is. For some perverse reason, in order to alleviate the ordinariness of life, I'd invented an SS father and an I.R.A. father and a Mäori mother to give my life some excitement and meaning!'

He walked to the Queen Street end of the square. The whole area was a sea of glittering, smashed glass. People wandered aimlessly around looking for signs of the riot not having happened. It was like waking and finding your wife or husband dead. The people looked as if they were all on tranquillisers – the kind that doctors give you when you're in shock. The tourist information centre was completely destroyed. All that remained was the concrete shell. The new glass-obsessed buildings of that area were all like the aftermath of an explosion. He looked back across the square and saw the headmistress and headmaster of this city, the Civic Administration Building and Auckland Central Police Station, looking unutterably sombre, not believing what their children had done. "We gave them everything!" they nodded to each other. Paul thought, what a stupid square this is, anyone who expected people to enjoy themselves under the constant gaze of the police, riot or no riot, had no idea of what people were like. In their little puritan offices they had designed a public play-pen where the big police can keep a constant watch. It made him sick!

Then he had a real pang of real fear! Maybe Hine and the baby didn't exist! If his father didn't exist, if Rangi and Tania didn't exist, then it was possible. He felt terrified. He thought he might be going mad. He almost slipped off into the heroin state of mind...Dr.Rampou in the Newmarket railway tunnel...graffiti by The Fly at station to station...every wave that reaches you...then one BONG! The Art Gallery clock told the city it was one o'clock. Paul Calvert looked over towards the Town Hall and saw an old man sitting on the third bench from the right. He also saw a black, late model Mercedes disappear down Queen Street and felt very exhausted all of a sudden. Walking slowly he moved towards the figure silently sitting on the seat. He said hello, and as Paul stood in front of this little old man it seemed impossible that he had been part of that murderous regime. He looked so frail that Paul could have killed him with one blow.

"Meine son," the older man said quietly, not able to suppress an underlying tremor in his voice. "My son, how long I've waited for this moment."

Paul felt repulsed by him and slightly scared. He didn't know what to say or do. Involuntarily he sat next to him. There was nothing else to do.

"I have been running, always running." The father seemed to want to talk and Paul Calvert was content to listen.

"I loved your mother. She was the most beautiful woman and she loved me Paul, and she loved Richard too. I loved her but it was no good. Having a Mäori woman in Germany at that time – it was useless. I pretended she was my guinea pig for racial experiments. I showed them my writings and the writings of Tregear about the Maoris being Aryan but it was no good. Oh, it looked all right on paper and they praised me for my theoretical work, but when they saw her dark skin and dark eyes they couldn't equate the two." Paul felt his father's genuine love for his mother and was confused.

"Of course," von Klagen continued, "Tregear's ideas were nonsense anyway, ja, but it was the only way I could get her released from the concentration camp. She had been picked up at the border travelling with Richard and he thought that was enough. But she was arrested for being one of the 'degenerate race.' Richard protested, but they told him 'You go on your way, Herr O'Hanlon, while you still can'. He arrived in Berlin most distraught and told me what had happened. His visa was for only two days, so I said I'd what I could do. I went to the camp where she was being held, and told them I was doing experiments and that I needed a dark woman. They all sniggered and made dirty comments, and brought me Mary O'Shea..."

"So you're saying that I'm not the result of some stupid experiment" Paul said to von Klagen. He felt so numb he could believe anything now.

"Nein! They were strange times ve vere in Paulus. And I was a member of the SS But your mother and I fell in love and we were lovers when Richard arrived back in Berlin. You see you couldn't have been the result of an experiment because you veren't even conceived until after the war, Ja!"

Paul Calvert felt a terrible sense of relief and an awareness of his own stupidity. Of course, he bad not been born until 1947. He thought to himself – 'wait till I get bold of Blunt, I'll throttle him.'

The old man continued, his accent becoming more and more German as his memories played before him.

"Vell, Paulus, it was dangerous for the three of us! I had told my superiors of my 'Mäori friend.' By the way, your mother vas a quarter Mäori from the Arawa people. Her own muter bad been living in the Tarawera village when the mountain erupted, but I don't know how much you know." Calvert was tempted to say, "I know nothing!" but was loath to turn this into a humorous occasion. He was actually beginning to like von Klagen and it was certainly good getting all this background knowledge of his parentage. However, Paul could see von Klagen felt uneasy, and when he asked him why, the older man said this was the first time he'd been in a public place since the 1950s.

"Anyway," he continued, "as the war got more intense, the Irish Government which was theoretically neutral, had pressure on them from the British and things got difficult for people like O'Hanlon. Although I loved Mary O'Shea I urged him to take her back to Ireland because I could only pretend about those experiments for so long, ja! Ha! I remember one night in Berlin, the last night the three of us were together." His old eyes lit up. "We were all at the Hotel Adlon, invited by Roy Calvert, an Englishman who was Richard's phoney brother."

Paul stopped him there and told him the account of that evening in Eggars senior's diary.

"Almost vord for vord!" He seemed amazed that Paul should know about this. "But there's one thing you don't know about und that is about the micro-dot hidden in the eyes of mein photograph!"

At this point Paul told von Klagen about his recent capture and torture by the neo-Nazi group and how they had wanted the photograph.

"But I didn't think microfilm had been invented by that stage," said Paul incredulously.

"It was a top-secret project and they thought it would be safe hidden in a picture of some insignificant SS Officer. As in so many things, the Nazis forgot about how people really are - they always thought in terms of robots or gods. That was, of course, their downfall!"

The two men talked on, the one talking, the other listening. Paul learned how his father got Richard O'Hanlon and Mary O'Shea out of Germany and how they intended to return to New Zealand under the name Calvert and become a normal couple, settle down and get married. Von Klagen was arrested by the Gestapo for losing the micro-dot plans, and was charged with treason against the Reich. However, he was released when it was found that his services and work were still needed in an increasingly desperate war situation. When the war ended he went underground.

"This!" He pointed to the smashed windows and shattered glass of Auckland's riots. "This is kid's stuff. You should haf been in Berlin or any German city at the end of the war, then you understand what a broken city is!"

Von Klagen had been captured by the Yanks in 1946 and was given the option of a public trial and certain execution, or working for the CIA.

"I chose the latter, I did not want to live particularly but I always hoped I vould see your mother again." And he did see her! In 1947 they spent a few weeks together in Hamburg. She had left New Zealand, having recently married Richard O'Hanlon, but not been able to settle back in the country herself. She had gone looking for von Klagen and had found him amidst the social and material rubble of post-war Europe.

"We had a wonderful few weeks together, of vich you are the result. One morning she got out of bed and said, 'I must go back to Richard, now.'" Von Klagen then told Paul that he was the one who had been following him in the black Mercedes. He had wanted to be sure it was his son. The older man had been in contact with his sister who was in Wellington – his brother and other sister were overseas. Paul asked him who he thought that big-wig Nazi was in the woolshed, but he didn't know.

"Some fanatic reliving the past. Mind you, Paul, if they ever got that photo it could be dangerous!"

Paul Calvert reached in his back pocket and pulled out the photograph he'd found on his dead mother and gave it to his father thinking the old man would be pleased to have it back as memento of the woman he had once loved.

"I can't believe it!" Von Klagen said when his son told him where he'd got it. "I just can't believe it! You don't know what this means. You could restore the Third Reich wif this - with the information here!" He was half struck by fear - half by awe. He had power again and it shook him.

The old man stood up as though he was about to address a Nuremberg Rally, it was frightening to watch. Paul wondered how many other people wandered the earth with this sense of sacred mission. Von Klagen was very quiet, as if Paul had evaporated from his life – he was a god, a robot, a slave to power, destined to rule over other slaves. He held the photo to his breast as if it was a source of power, like a crucifix, a pounamu. He gained Supernatural Strength from this symbol of past glories and future power.

A single shot rang out across the square. Paul's father fell dead at his feet. Sirens wailed and cops came running from the police station. Paul Calvert was treated for shock by the police doctor at the scene and discharged. Wilkinson whisked him away in a car to the police station. A few hours later Wilkinson came to see Paul Calvert.

"A silver bullet through the heart, an SS assassination" said the inspector. "I tried to warn you, Calvert." It was funny hearing his familiar name.

"It's probably for the best," Paul said. He asked Wilco about the photograph.

"He must have been holding it near his heart. It was completely destroyed, we only found a few fragments - no micro data or anything like that. We haven't found who did it yet, probably left the country. We found a fold-up rifle next to a clarinet case on top of one of the high rise buildings – a one-shot affair. We checked all the wind ensembles in Auckland and other orchestras and found one who had a clarinet player, Martin Wilhelm, who left two hours ago to return to Germany. He's our prime suspect. He must have set up the assassination with a local hit man. It's in the hands of Interpol now. We've still got nothing conclusive on those chaps who got you. I expect we won't be hearing much from any Nazis or neo-Nazis in Auckland for a while now."

They talked on for an hour or so, then Wilkinson dropped Paul home – Hine came running out to meet him, she had heard about the shooting on the radio and thought that he'd been hit. To save an argument Paul said he'd been in hospital until now and couldn't get near a phone. The truth was that the first instinctive thing he'd felt when he left police medic's care was to contact her, needing to have her near him so that she knew he was all right, and to get her strength by being with her, just holding her in his arms. But when he got to the cop shop Wilco and he were talking so intensely that he simply forgot to phone her. Paul remembered the last time when he 'simply forgot' with Hine and thought it wiser to go for the little white lie.

EPILOGUE

The next few weeks were quite eventful in a domestic way. Hine and Paul decided to leave Auckland. He had a bit of a run-in with her father when they told her family she was pregnant. But they ended up going to the pub and getting drunk together. Her insisted that he didn't want his daughter to marry a 'bloody Päkehä' and when Paul told him firmly he was also from Te Arawa, still getting used to the idea himself, her father looked at him fiercely as if he was going to eat him. Then he said, "That's worse!" There was silence for awhile and then they both roared with laughter and bought more drink.

Paul Te Ariki Calvert often felt the dull thud of the bullet going into his father's heart as he stood beside him in Aotea Square. Often he woke at night having dreamt that he had been hit. Hinengaro would talk him out of his panic and he would go to sleep safely entwined in her arms. At this time Paul took on the name his father told him his mother wanted to call him as a second name, Te Ariki, so he and Hinengaro both now had more palpable Mäori identities. They decided to go to Wellington to stay with Rina, Hine's sister. Then they would think about finding a place in the country and set up house in time for the baby. While in Wellington he would see if he could find his own sister. It would be good to get back with his family and share all the knowledge he'd gained concerning their mother and fathers.

Also, now that Paul Te Ariki Calvert was about to start a new generation with Hinengaro Te Riro i He he felt an instinctive pull towards the whänau. He had heard that places around Dunedin were very nice and also north of Gisborne. As Hinengaro and he discussed possible destinations for our home Paul felt that it didn't matter that much as long as they were together. One place he wanted to go at some stage was around the Rotorua area, to find out about his Arawa family, but it would be many years hence before that could occur.

Hinengaro and Paul Te Ariki were married just before they left Auckland. The next evening they were sitting in our seats on the Northerner. As the train pulled out from Platform One of Auckland Station they waved a last good-bye to Skids, Golly and Hine's parents. Her mum had given Paul a koha, a piece of pounamu to wear around his neck as a symbol of strength and protection. It had been handed down through generations to all the male heads of the first family to the next generation. He felt the mana of the stone heavy around his neck and hoped he would be worthy of it.

They had Te Arohanui, Hinengaro's young sister with them. She was also going to stay with Rina to give their parents a bit of time together to sort out their relationship, rather than the yearly merry-go-round involved in going up North. Rewi had rung earlier to say good-bye and to tell them that Liz had gone into hospital and would give birth anytime now, which is why he couldn't come and see them off.

It was a beautiful evening as the train picked up speed and headed out along the embankment towards Orakei and the pohutukawa trees were in full bloom along Tamaki Drive. It seemed only hours since that morning he'd arrived back from dreamland. Paul Te Ariki looked at a telegram Golly had put in his hand as they boarded the train. Paul laughed when he read "Good luck you two, see you next time you want to know about your family, love Tony and Cara." Paul showed it to Hine and she smiled and kissed him. "We on our way at last, e. You O.K. Te Aroha?" The little girl said she was. She was sitting in the single seat on the other side of the aisle reading a comic. As the train headed south after stopping briefly at Papakura, Auckland was almost out of Paul Te Ariki Calvert's veins. He looked out the window and saw the red earth, barely discernible as the darkness descended. He looked out and saw high rolls of cloud bringing a lightning storm to Auckland. He loved this place and felt sad. He knew this city that didn't know itself, but he looked at Hinengaro sitting next to him with their child inside her and he knew they had to leave.

Paul Te Ariki remembered an old Māori greeting which he turned into a farewell to Auckland. "E Tamaki e, e noho ra, E Tamaki-makau Rau – e!" he whispered. The sound of the train wheels rushing in the wind as they passed out of Auckland's border sounded as though words were forming in answer to his good-bye.

"Ka whakahoki koe, e hoa. Ka whakahoki kia Tamaki-makau rau."

"I know I will be back," he replied.

Paul was tired and happy as he drifted off to sleep, his head resting on Hinengaro's shoulder as the train rushed into the night.

www.ingramcontent.com/pod-product-compliance
Lightning Source LLC
Chambersburg PA
CBHW070533130626
46555CB00003B/1392